ESSAYS AND STUDIES
1977

ESSAYS AND STUDIES
1977

BEING VOLUME THIRTY OF THE NEW SERIES
OF ESSAYS AND STUDIES COLLECTED FOR
THE ENGLISH ASSOCIATION

BY W. MOELWYN MERCHANT

HUMANITIES PRESS

ATLANTIC HIGHLANDS, N. J.

© The English Association 1977

All rights reserved. No part of this publication may be reproduced, stored in a retrieval system, or transmitted, in any form or by any means, electronic, mechanical, photocopying, recording or otherwise, without the prior permission of John Murray (Publishers) Ltd, 50 Albemarle Street, London WIX 4BD

Printed in Great Britain by
Cox &Wyman Ltd, London, Fakenham and Reading

0-391-00701-7

Preface

An introductory word may be permitted to a somewhat unusual volume of *Essays and Studies*. One conviction is shared in common by all the contributors: that literary insights are deepened by invoking the methods and techniques of other disciplines: archaeology, music, fine art, theology. This is in no way to disparage or devalue the 'purity of the word on the page', to write off the 'New Criticism' in America or 'close reading' in Great Britain; it is simply to say that some of the old disciplines (like theology) or the craft of the new (like that of the film-maker) may give us unexpected light. And this is not a matter of 'content' but truly of 'discipline' – for we have learnt their indivisibility.

Finally, the critics happily take their place beside the creative artists, who in turn are revealed as critics. The painter, Josef Herman, speaks critically from the heart of his craftsmanship; the playwright, Christopher Fry, writes from the core of his struggle with seemingly intractable material. Many more friends could have been invoked at these frontiers but space is limited.

W.M.M.

Contents

Heroes, Heroism and Heroic Literature

MICHAEL SWANTON

ATTEMPTS to understand the literature of the European Heroic Age by way of the comparative method conventional for almost a century have involved the analysis of cultures chronologically and geographically so disparate that only the lowest common factors emerge. And descriptive accounts of the figure of the hero himself prove equally inadequate for much the same reason. But changing perspectives in our understanding of the period open up possible avenues of approach which might clarify the nature of the literature by way of the social aspirations it reflects. The literature in question emerged in north and west Europe during the fourth and fifth centuries, and was thus coterminous with the collapse of the Roman Empire in the west. It is this fact that has bedevilled the question for so long. Generations of classically-educated critics, their imaginations haunted by this catastrophe, have thought of the fall of Rome as a radical divide, a cultural watershed separating order and chaos, civilization and barbarism, urban sophistication and 'dark age' superstition. But such simple dichotomies had no firmer basis than the imagination of their proponents. Current reassessment of critical documentary sources, together with cognate disciplines such as archaeology, philology and the history of ideas, emphasizes the evolutionary rather than revolutionary aspects of this period. Recognition of the resemblance rather than the dissimilarity of contiguous cultures in the north-west at this time makes accessible a substantial body of material evidence which, when thoroughly considered, may help clarify our understanding of the heroic phenomenon.

The great land-takings of the Migration Age merely confirmed and accelerated tendencies long present in European society: its political and economic fragmentation and consequent social and intellectual turmoil. In fact Roman civilization in its extreme Hellenistic manifestation had disappeared with the civil strife of the third century. With decay of central government the great households, already self-sufficient economically, assumed increasing localized military responsibility. As the disaffected flocked to the local potentiores for protection, there developed within the limes a pattern of patronatus and clientela not markedly dissimilar from the familiar Germanic comitatus. In Britain, at least, shadowy kingdoms of a pre-Roman type had emerged over a generation before the official end of central administration: ephemeral institutions depending for their existence on the reputation of a single man, described variously as *rex, tyrannus, princeps, dux,* etc. This period is characterized by the reoccupation of ancient pre-Roman hilltop strongholds, some built entirely new, most refurbished, modified and reduced in size. The massive fortification of Cadbury-Camelot, Somerset, implies the existence of concerted regional organization during at least part of this phase, and must represent the base for an army that was large by the standards of the time, and the court of a military leader of some status—if not the historical Arthur then an Arthur figure of some kind. But most, like Castle Dore in Cornwall, the abode of Mark/Cunomorus and the original locale for the Tristan and Iseult story, were much smaller, designed to be easily defended by a comitatus of, say, between thirty and a hundred men. No doubt such forts would serve not only to defend the local population, but also ensure the personal protection of the tyrannus and his retinue from their 'subjects'. They represent the strongholds of a local military and political élite, at least some of whom seem to have sponsored a revival of paganism at this time. Almost all exhibit aristocratic material tastes, marked by a variety of luxury goods imported from southern Gaul and the Mediterranean. But if the occasion of this development is clear, the origins of those who set themselves up as local tyranni are shrouded in mystery. They may have come from the last of the 'Roman' aristocracy, rich landowners like the man who saw that the rock-cut defences of Bokerly Dyke, laid out to defend an imperial estate in north Dorset in the fourth century, were refurbished into the fifth; or from the urban gentry, like the municeps Gratian, probably from Verulamium, who was briefly fêted by the army in Britain in its last days. Dispossessed noblemen from any part of the province, immigrant Irish or even Picts may have taken advantage of the final collapse of centralized administration to seize lands and power. Some certainly were native princes like Cunedda who came with eight sons from Manau Guotodin, glorying in fine-sounding Roman military titles, to found a dynasty in Gwynedd. The 'Celtic' interior of Britain was in as considerable a state of ethnic and social turmoil as the Teutonic-settled east. Such unstable conditions must have allowed considerable social mobility, and it is possible that other tyranni represented a quite new ruling class, perhaps rising Spartacus-like from the ranks of former native bailiffs. It is scarcely surprising that it was this society that should give rise to the strongly active Pelagian ethic of self-reliance, with its insistence on the exercise of independent will, its belief that ultimately all men would be judged strictly on their merits. The Empire may have gone forever—no matter; individuals might look to their own salvation; vigorous local resistance was both possible and desirable; it was evident that by his own exertions a man might save himself in this world—and the next.

Among those—Roman or barbarian in origin—who considered themselves still part of the Empire, two broad attitudes emerged: one party yearning for stability, nostalgic for centralized authority, whose only hope was reunion with the eastern Empire and the regimentation and oriental despotism that that involved; while others sought to come to terms with the practical realities of local devolution. In the north-west provinces 'Roman' society had long lived side by side with 'barbarian'. It had been imperial policy to settle groups of more or less independent Celts and Teutons within the limes to exercise a quasi-military role. The army itself was increasingly Germanized from the third century, until eventually the most outstanding military figures of the later days of the Empire were barbarians like the Vandal Stilicho. The prestige the barbarian leaders began to enjoy in the eyes of much of the Roman world was matched by increasing self-assurance on their part, their sense of individuality marked by their retaining

German names instead of Latinizing them as former recruits into the Roman army had done. They acceded to the highest rank, both of military command and consulship. The Emperor Arcadius took into marriage the daughter of one of the more successful Frankish mercenaries, Arbogast *comes* at Trier. And young men of fashion commonly affected Teuton dress and hair-styles, although this was forbidden in Rome itself. Of course there were aristocrats like the Gallo-Roman Sidonius Apollinaris who would exhibit the social prejudice natural to them, mocking their neighbours' croaking speech, their strange customs, even their unusual odour, while admiring and relying upon their courage and vigorous independence. A generation later there was already a Gallo-Roman fashion for adopting Teutonic names. And at the battle of Vouillé in 507 between Visigoths and Franks, Gallo-Romans would fight bravely on both halves, Sidonius' own grandson being among those who fought by the side of the defeated Visigothic leader after his own men had fled. Some 'Romans' seem to have gone completely native. The wealthy businessman whom Priscus encountered at the court of Attila, who had distinguished himself in Hunnish military service and considered his present life preferable to his past, was by no means unique. In devolution first local and then personal loyalties assume paramount importance. During the phase of British recovery following the battle of Mons Badonicus, the founding West Saxon war-leader Cerdic bore a Celtic name; and at least one of his successors, Cædwalla, who came out of obscurity at the head of his comitatus to fight for the kingdom, also bore a Celtic name. As late as 784 a British hostage attached to the comitatus of Cynewulf was prepared to fight to the death if necessary to avenge his Saxon patron's death, rather than take the opportunity to escape when it was offered him. The war-band of a Hengest or a Cerdic may have contained a host of warriors who shared little in common save a deep personal commitment to their leader and mutual dependence on his prowess. It is not insignificant that the first English poet we can identify, Cædmon, also had a Celtic name. Ethnic blurring was a natural consequence of the *Völkerwanderung*, as nations shifted, driven by economic and political necessities, absorbing and absorbed by others, leaving remnants of their peoples as isolated pockets on the way—a feature that seems to have been as true for British and Gallic as for Teutonic tribes. Archaeological evidence shows that on the eve of the great land-takings, the Anglo-Saxons were already a mixed and mongrel people. The considerable confusion of the documentary record merely reflects actuality. It should not have puzzled the Beowulfian critics that the Geat Weohstan could be regarded as a Scylfing prince, fighting on behalf of the Swede Onela, the Geats' implacable enemy, or that at the end of his life Beowulf (perhaps reflecting his literary alter ego Bjarki) should be described as a Scylding champion. The ethnic dissociation of European heroic society is reflected in the non-national subject matter of its literature. It is significant that the hero of the first great English poem is not an Englishman but a Geat who undertakes adventures in Denmark, while the Arthurian 'matter of Britain' was best preserved in France. In the far north the oldest stories are not those of Scandinavian heroes but Goths, Burgundians and Huns.

Just as the open society which allowed for the rise of an heroic age emerged in the hiatus of authority which yawned between the breakdown of imperial administration and its restoration in feudal form at the close of the eighth century, so it lay geographically in a broad band either side of the old limes: a region of fluid social movement in the frontier provinces of north and west Europe, rather than deep in the heartlands either of Mediterranean empire or Germano-Slavic barbarism. Heroic society properly speaking is not characteristic of the relatively stable agrarian economies of interior. Neither the Finno-Ugric farthest north nor isolated Ireland ever developed a meaningful heroic literature, scarcely evolving beyond the sacral epic where ultimate human motives rise above the peasant interests of abduction or cattle-stealing only to be distorted by myth and magic. The general nature of the open society which fostered the heroic virtues of self-reliance and active initiative is well known: a warfare society in which a man could rise to prominence by wisdom or courage, but might retain his position by example in the van of battle rather than by authority *de jure*. At the same time freedom from traditional external restraints, whether those of imperial bureaucracy or tribal authority, meant that the only source of censure or approval is reduced to that of the *comites*, who by definition exist only in their estimation of the *dux*. Power consists in the ability to attract and maintain a large and enthusiastic comitatus. In consequence, the mere weight of a leader's reputation would of itself often virtually decide the issue of war. The *dux* both generates and confirms his reputation by open-handed generosity of an order which degrades neither the giver nor the recipient, and by ostentatious hospitality, a prominent part of which included the entertainment of poets.

The role of the poet is central to heroic society, recording and rehearsing its ideology. Their professional status was guaranteed by early Celtic and Germanic legal codes. Some attached themselves to a particular hero, others were peripatetic, of which the types are Deor and Widsith respectively. It is not insignificant that these are mere pseudonyms. Their verse is necessarily anonymous since its function is to serve his patron's reputation, not his own. His client's urgent priority was for fame in his own lifetime. Like Hroðgar's scop, he will speak of heroes of the past as well as the present; in due course, if his song is successful, it will enter the popular repertoire and its subject will become part of the traditional stock of heroic legends. Because heroic poetry originates in the need to celebrate men with an originally purely local reputation, it is scarcely surprising that so many heroes of this literature are unknown to history. It is presumably a matter of chance that the founding war-leader Clovis, whose picturesque exploits occupy so many pages of contemporary chronicles, should be unremembered in verse. But the poet did not choose his subject necessarily because he was an effective figure on the world stage, but for what he quite personally achieved or endured. Historical verse as such belongs to a later age. The most momentous events of the age—the fall of Rome or the defeat of Attila—seem never to have caught the poetic imagination. Heroic verse is concerned with the fate of the individual rather than that of his nation, although the two are sometimes linked. While their lives are often played out against a background of significant events, the exploits recorded are not in themselves such as to affect the fate of nations. The protracted and savage wars between the Goths and Huns are reduced to a personal quarrel between the two half-brothers Angantýr and Hlǫðr Heiðreksson. The great struggle in which the Huns destroyed Gundahari's Burgundians in 437 is represented as merely a family dispute between Atli and Gunnar and their respective comitatus, as though it had no greater historical moment than the mutual decimation of a little-known group of Frisians and Half-Danes at Finnsburh where a closely similar situation occurred. Significant events are disregarded or reduced to the scene of an individual prince's hall. Although in fact armies of many thousands took the field, the heroic unit of reference is the comitatus. The reduction in scale serves to enhance the heroic integrity because the critical issues are unobscured by larger external affairs.

While the names of the heroes, like the stories attached to them, undergo strange mutations when recorded in different countries at different times, the exhaustive studies of scholars like the late Kemp Malone show there is no reason to doubt that the persons described, if not all the exploits attributed to them, have some historical substance. Of course the poet shaped his material to meet artistic and other ends. Historical events and personalities are conflated, transferred, simplified. Relative chronologies, even simple relationships, are unimportant. Theodoric is placed at the court of Eormenric, Maenwyn at that of Maelgwn, although in fact the parties were separated by a century in either case. Widsith's claims to have visited the courts of heroes who lived centuries apart simply underlines the point. The dynastic relationships suggested in *Beowulf* are incompatible with later Scandinavian tradition, and any effort to piece together a coherent history of the Germanic north based on this material is naturally frustrated. Historians who suppose incidental confusion rather than fundamental irrelevance, misunderstand the poet's premise. It is truely irrelevant whether Beowulf returned to eventually become king in Geatland, or under the name Bjarki remained at Heorot to live and die a favoured berserkr of Hroðgar's successor, Hrólfr Kraki/Hroþulf.

The verse of the Heroic Age is clearly interpretative, the literary persona diverging from the historic one at a relatively early stage in its existence. The inventive element in the poem is important; heroes are often attached to, even identified with, a tribal myth of much greater antiquity. The respective stages are recognizable in *Beowulf*. The poet's primary function is seen in the praise of the brave defence of Heorot, enhancing the hero in question by comparison with a hero of former times whose exploits have already become legendary. The plot of *Beowulf* as a whole represents a developed stage of the simple encomium, in which the hero is identified with larger national myths: the troll-slaying berserkr and dragon-slaying king. (It was at an equivalent stage and similar date that Arthur became the subject of those aetiological myths of South Wales and the West Country which Nennius appends to his *Historia*.) But in its final form *Beowulf* marks yet a third stage; writing at the very close of the European Heroic Age, the author has left a measured and highly sophisticated critique of heroic society as a whole and the role of leadership within it. Even at so late a stage, however, the world of romance is far away. The protagonist of heroic literature stalks across a real world which the poet is at some pains to delineate. Physical details are introduced not for the sake of decoration but for the verisimilitude they impart. The scene is no never-never land of fairy-tale wonder, but a material world which can be recognized by the audience as its own. 'Once upon a time' is a formula for irrelevance. There is no point in praising a hero who could never have lived. Our native belief that giants once lived in the world derives not from imagination but from experience. With the passage of time the hero acquires a more gigantic stature, magnified, distorted even, by the twilight through which he moves. But he never appears supernatural rather than merely superhuman. The hero may possess remarkable attributes, but they are not magical. Beowulf's berserkr tendencies are well illustrated in the perfectly credible, if heroic, account of his crushing to death the Frankish champion Dæghrefn before escaping across the Rhine bearing a large quantity of looted war-gear. It is merely an extension of this which sets him to fight the hideous underwater trolls—and it may have seemed appropriate that such a man should have ended his life facing a dragon rather than a human foe. But although a violent and successful warrior, outmatching ordinary mortals, the poet avoids any temptation to endow him with supernatural properties. There is no mention of the shape-shifting stories which so easily attach themselves to such men at other times or in other societies. Fictional mechanisms such as disguises, dreams, speaking animals, are all set aside as the province of romance. Neither God nor the gods motivate the action. The underlying assumption is that man himself has sufficient claim to our interest without recourse to supernatural powers on his behalf. Heroic poetry is concerned with the possibilities open to the human spirit, even if the standards set should seem too impossibly high to emulate. It is avowedly unimaginative because of its claims to be true.

The circumstances of the hero's death are subject to particular scrutiny, since this represents the culmination of his heroic career. It is interesting because of its very inevitability. And because common to all men, the fact of death is one element with which the audience may readily identify. The manner of his death raises in most piquant and critical terms the motives and standards of conduct which underly his achievement. Here more than anywhere it is the poet's function to transform the commonplace realities of misconduct and failure. The heroic ethos will allow neither Eormenric's despair and consequent suicide at the approach of the Huns, nor the more lurid haemorrhage of Attila's wedding-night. These might be recorded accurately by the cold eye of the classical historian, but the heroic poet brought both events into alignment with the favoured Finnsburh model: death through vengeance arising from the dilemma of divided loyalties. Nor are heroes slain in the random slaughter we know to have been the reality of a medieval battlefield—acknowledged only later with *Maldon*, where Byrhtnoð would meet his death unceremoniously at the hands of an anonymous ceorl. The death of a hero was best undergone confronting an opponent worthy of him; any less would detract from his stature. The greatness and heroic virtue of one's enemy is readily acknowledged. Political cause and effect are ignored; blame or praise for any issue are apportioned not in relation to external factors but in proportion to the individual's response to the situation which arises. It was Augustine or Jerome from a safe distance who would denounce Attila, *flagellum dei*, not those who encountered him face to face. No human enemy will yet be identified with Anti-Christ; the assumption of his brutality or inferiority belongs to a later age. It is this necessity which lies behind the many tales of single combat, real or supposed, of which we hear. And this too may account for the custom of ascribing one's own heroic deeds to the leader. Thus in *Beowulf* Hygelac can be described as the slayer of Ongenþeow, although elsewhere in the poem this is specifically acknowledged to be the work of Wulf and Eofor. Of course a hero in his own right, or an aspirant to heroic status, could not easily subscribe to this fiction, although the comitatus nexus might be satisfied by making over the material rewards of his exploit—characteristically the arms and armour of a defeated foe—to his leader. Sometimes only the greatest rewards were commensurate with the exploit in question —in Beowulf's case amounting to half the kingdom. Hygelac is fortunate that Beowulf should prove so unusually loyal to his leader's dynasty—at once the ideal and the natural development of the comitatus ethic, the only possible resolution of its inherently centrifugal tendencies. The existence of too close a contender for public estimation underlines the tensions always present in heroic society. In the Cædmonian *Genesis* the pride which causes Satan's fall is represented as envy of God's sole supremacy and a consuming desire for an independent hall and comitatus.

The poet's idealized fiction concealed and transformed a sordid proclivity for mutual extermination, illustrated so well by the heroic but dismal facts of the *putsch* at Merton in 784. The vigour and courageous energy so respected by commentators like Tacitus, could assume less admirable qualities when unconfined by any restraint. Irresponsible power often defends itself by cruelty, and the fact that, far from becoming merely despicable, the great men of this society still arouse our admiration and awe, is due to the nature of the heroic ethic. In the absence of a stable economy, the warfare society is savagely self-consuming, needing a constant flow of loot on which to feed. The premium placed on personal success meant that fratricidal wars were inevitable. And when stability depended on the survival of a single charismatic individual, it is hardly surprising that kingdoms should rise and fall in quick succession, whole nations often disappearing without trace. Heroic poetry celebrates mere episodes in the lives of men caught up in a constant process of disintegration and dissolution. The sudden reversal of fortune which is an ever-present theme of heroic literature had its model in reality, in the total eclipse not merely of an individual comitatus but of the greatest European powers: the destruction of the Hunnish empire after the death of Attila, of the Vandals after Genseric or the Ostrogoths after Theodoric. Renown, as Tacitus remarked, is easier won among perils, and the greatest heroes emerge not in the heyday of a culture but at its end. Beowulf and Arthur, close contemporaries, emerge in the twilight of their civilizations, the sole rallying-point, the only hope of the nation in the throes of its historical destruction. According to Cassiodorus, the Ostrogothic hero Gensimundus, who reigned in the ruins after Eormenric's empire had been destroyed by the Huns, was widely celebrated in poetry, but has left only his name to history. These heroes strut out their brief lives in a misty age which endows them with both magnitude and poignancy, theirs being an heroic task because hopeless, defying an apparently inevitable consequence.

It is the facts of reality which impart the elegiac tone that pervades all heroic verse. When Gelimer, last king of the Vandals, was facing final defeat by Herulian mercenaries in Byzantine pay, he asked their leader to send him a harp with which to accompany a song he had composed on his own misfortune. We are not told the content of Gelimer's dirge, but he could not have failed to recall that less than a hundred years earlier his predecessors dominated Europe, sacked Rome itself and founded the singularly wealthy kingdom of Carthage. Led in triumph with his comitatus through the streets of Byzantium, he is described repeating to himself: 'Vanity of vanities, all is vanity'. It is the burden of *The Wanderer* that a man must experience his share of winters in the world before he comes to realize his part in the transitory nature of things, and the quietude that understanding brings. The image of the ruined hall which underlies and completes the frequent 'ubi sunt' passages in heroic verse was no mere literary device. Abandoned and ruined buildings overgrown by brambles were a common feature of the European landscape during these years. The image found in *Beowulf* or the Exeter Book elegies recurs as naturally in the Welsh lament for Urien's Rheged or a Gallo-Roman account of the fall of the house of the Thuringian princess Radegunde. Explicitly or implicitly contrasted with the former glories of princely life, this is a penitential theme. The Pelagian author of the *Carmen de Providentia* will turn from the contemplation of ruined villa and empty fields to consider the defeat of evil in his own soul. The physical devastation of the world is taken to be an ever-present witness to its moral degeneration. While deeply mistrusting its institutions, which they saw only in burdensome decay, the new world was nostalgic for the technological fruits of the old—the weapons or walling which with good reason might be ascribed to giants whose like would never be seen again. It is an ancient sword-hilt bearing a picture of the giants who warred against God and were thus destroyed that Hroðgar uses as the 'text' for the sermon which forms the structural and thematic hinge of *Beowulf*. It is a sermon on mutability, and the inevitable decline of any hero in face of this fact; either violent death will come to him or, much more dreadful, the decay of old age will frustrate the heroic impetus more tragically. The old king wept when he remembered the exploits of his youth, just as the minstrels who told of Attila's deeds roused some in spirit, but caused older men to weep since, enfeebled by age, their courageous spirit must perforce remain unsatisfied.

There is no doubt but that one of the functions of such poems was to inspire emulation; the audience is constantly exhorted: 'Learn from this ... thus ought a man to do ...' The early Germani chanted the praises of heroes as they advanced into battle, and the songs Aneurin describes the British warriors singing as they rode into defeat at Catraeth were probably of the same order. The only specific information we have as to the likely nature of such battle-songs comes from the eleventh century:

before Hastings the *Song of Roland* and before Stikelstad the *Bjarkamál* (concerning the disastrous attack on Lejre/Heorot in which Hrólfr Kraki and his comitatus, including Bjarki/Beowulf, all die). It was apparently not the glorious victory but the glories of defeat that best suited the heroic temper. The songs thought appropriate during the celebrations following Grendel's defeat were said to be 'true and sad'.

Roland and the *Bjarkamál* are songs of defeat, but not defeatism. Indeed, the heroic posture depends upon the possibility of defeat, which is at once acknowledged and defied. An awareness of the universality of mutability should not be mistaken for mere pessimism or a sense of futility, although in a closed society like the Mediterranean it would engender fatalism, degrading the activity of the individual will. The fundamental assumption is that man's will, because free, may prove superior to the fate which sooner or later must destroy him—a dynamic ethic of active courage, asserting human capacity for achievement unaided by supernatural means, whether divine or merely magical. The hero's role is to develop his potential to the greatest his *wyrd* will allow, living each day as if it were his last. At any time a reversal of fortune might occur: '*wyrd* goes ever as it will'. The hero inhabits a world of risks and decisions, and our admiration is aroused by the unflinching spirit with which he confronts the realities of that world, attempting tasks beyond the imagination, or at least the abilities, of the rank and file. The dangerous environment does not of itself engender heroism. Unlike the Roman, the 'barbarian' was not necessarily prepared to participate in violence for its own sake; Saxon captives would commit mutual suicide rather than engage in the gratuitous violence of gladiatorial contests. Heroism in the technical sense is not to be confused with bravery, nor yet recklessness. Tacitus said of the Germanic *comites* that they would debate at a time that cuts out pretence but decide at a time that precludes mistake. When the *beot* coincides with action, heroism is the result: the boast achieved. The hero's *beot* is a defiant exercise of will in face of what will sooner or later prove his downfall, the *wyrd* he is incapable of postponing. *Wyrd* is a sophisticated concept, corresponding exactly to neither 'fate' nor 'fortune', but meaning rather 'course of events, that which will come about'. Whether or not this is pre-ordained in some way is strictly irrelevant to the moral issue. The hero must strive for *lof* and *dom* in the face of whatever odds he happens to encounter. Eventually the odds must prove too great; in the meantime the fact that *lif is læne* was no excuse for hesitancy or despair which, as Beowulf asserts in at least his early life and in the advice he gives, is the enemy of heroism. This anti-defeatist assertion of heroic free will found its moral counterpart in the Christian world in Pelagius' insistence that man ought properly to be considered master of his own fate, defying secular and ecclesiastical bureaucracies in striving after perfection—the unrealizability of which should not be admitted although witnessed on all sides. The heroic act, religious or secular, consists in the progression: *posse, velle, esse*. In so far as God will intervene, it is to help those who help themselves: '*yðelice syþðan he eft astod*' (*Beowulf*, 1556). Beowulf's three great fights mark a progression in our understanding of the source of the hero's power: from total self-reliance, through closer questioning of the adequacy of his sole strength and recognition that God provides the necessary resources to the right man; and finally in old age falling into despair thinking that he must have offended God in some way. Beowulf himself contains the dilemma of heroic society—the need for a strong man, and yet uncertainty as to the source of his authority. The poem is full of ambiguity and unease at the condition of heroic society, and already anticipates the clerical response of Alcuin—the notion that man's power is greatest when acknowledging that he is merely the channel through which God's power flows into the world, and the consequent feudal ideology of *auctoritas dei gratia*. The hero's self-awareness, his recognition of the nature of the world and his own part in it, is easily mistaken by lesser men for lack of due humility. 'It is no man's measure but mine alone to display heroism,' says Beowulf before dying. He believes for an instant—the moment of *beot*—that he may still overcome. It is an excess of herosim which denies the essentially reciprocal nature of comitatus society. But, a child of his age, he knows no other course. Wiglaf at least is resigned to the fact that often many men must suffer for the will of one man, with its implication that somehow we must needs become our own heroes if we are to survive. The active ideal of self-reliance is an élitist and isolative one, and ultimately alien to the open society which engenders it. In practice the discord that Grendel and his kind represent is always ready to intrude. The 'adventurous act' leaves its record in a genuinely ethical literature which, albeit fragmentary and mutilated, may still arouse our admiration and awe. The conflagration kindled by the barbarian incendiaries of a devastated world could, as Arnold Toynbee remarked, make a slum look like Valhalla.

By the same token, the heroic Pelagian ideal was naturally attractive in aristocratic circles; this phase in the insular church was characterized by the lengthy catalogue of British and Saxon princely saints. The saint stepped easily into the hero's niche; the warfare of the *miles spiriti* was conducted with heroic determination. Faustus exhorts his community at Lerins as though they were an armed camp 'met not for peace and security but for a struggle and a conflict . . . we have embarked on a war'. Whether or not the schismatic movements of these times caused or were caused by imperial dissolution, there can be no doubt but that they reflect the social and political separatism of the provinces. And it is no coincidence that whereas Africa and the East were characterized by Donatism and the monophysite controversy respectively, northwest Europe, the seat of heroic society, witnessed the emergence of the Pelagian movement. While it is, and was, doubtful in the extreme whether the attitude represented by Pelagius should ever have been considered heretical, it certainly reflects a religious complexion quite at odds with the authoritarian temper of the centralist Mediterranean church.

The theological and historical progress of the controversy is now sufficiently well known not to need restatement. As so often, it is accusation and counter-accusation rather than the rational truth of the matter that reveals the nature of contemporary attitudes. The clear issues and simple decisions of the Great Persecution were long past. For something over a generation Christianity had been the religion of court and official life. And with this had come the problem of nominalism on the one hand, as wealthy families lapsed into conformity, and on the other an inevitable blurring of the judicial and ecclesiastical roles of the clergy. The bishopric of Rome was already a prize to be won, and church affairs already the subject of considerable violence. It was this world that had to accommodate the undeniable fact of imperial collapse. For the conservative Mediterranean party the fall of Rome was deeply traumatic. In the face of social and political instability they would cling blindly to the familiar. While hoping that eventually the *civitas dei* might prove independent of the fate of worldly states, their doctrinal and institutional absolutism meant that they could not, if they would, propose any other model than that of the imperial bureaucracy. Others, especially those living in the north-west provinces, like the fifth-century Gallo-Roman realist Salvian, were less sanguine that the Empire could be salvaged. *De gubernatione dei* traces a process of gradual accommodation to the new conditions, acknowledging the cleansing discomfort of the social and spiritual readjustment the northern world required. The centrifugal tendencies of the provinces were present in Rome itself, where certain leading aristocratic families, living in their own palaces or on estates outside the city, formed a pattern of isolated groups; responding to Paul's injunction to work out their own salvation with fear and trembling, they favoured an ascetic life, each striving to achieve a degree of spiritual perfection that differed from that of the rank and file. It was in this world that Pelagius made his appearance, lawyer and influential lay preacher moving in aristocratic circles, concerned to work out the challenge of Christian living for the layman, believing intensely that the health of the church existed only in the health of its individual members and emphasizing the independence of the individual within the overall equity of God. Pelagius was no theologian, but a fiercely pragmatic moralist. He was constantly exasperated by the ineffectual character of mere nominalists and their feeble complaint that they were hindered by the weakness of their human nature. And when he found this apparently systematically excused by one of the most influential church writers of the day, he was moved to anger. Augustine's over-epigrammatic *Da quod iubes et iube quod vis* with all it implied, he took to be mystical nonsense, an unacceptable retreat into hopelessly fatalistic determinism, an insidious consequence of the African's Manichaean heritage. It would degrade the individual to the role of an impotent puppet, sapping the will to self-improvement and actually encouraging the nominalist to lapse into the moral torpor of a confirmed invalid. It must have seemed a theology of depravity and despair; the negation of human freedom denied not only the dignity of man but the goodness of God. Man is called upon to be perfect; he will not, of course, achieve that perfection. But God is not capricious and does not command the impossible; 'ought' implies 'can'. The universality of sin and its inevitability—an inevitability which cannot be conceded—ensures that the life of the *integri christiani* is an heroic assertion, his commitment a moment of *beot* affirming the heroic progression: *posse, velle, esse.* The controversy was never conventionally dogmatic; Augustine and Pelagius displayed an unusually deep personal respect for one another. Their dispute arose from a conflict of priorities rather than doctrine. The protagonists simply represented the expectations of their differing cultures. The African monk's unilinear logic reduced his awareness of human frailty to a cosmic pattern into which the mere business of practical living must be accommodated in some way. The British lawyer and layman, fiercely individualist, was concerned first and foremost to construct a pattern of life acceptable to divine justice, a man's fate lying in his own hands. As in the secular sphere, the dominant assertion of free will commonly gave rise to accusations of pride.

Theological debate proved ineffective; in the event no general consensus of church opinion could be found to condemn Pelagius as heretical. The ultimate sanction was political rather than doctrinal. The diversity of 'protestant' free thought represented by the Pelagians clearly could not be tolerated by an authoritarian regime facing its last days. Any movement that opened up divisions in society was inimical to the monolithic interests of both church and state. It was the renewed threat from heroic society with which the Pelagians had so much in common that led to their downfall. Some of the most influential of Pelagius' aristocratic supporters were accused of collaborating with the barbarian invader, and agitation on the part of the African party eventually secured an edict from the Emperor Honorius banishing all Pelagians and confiscating their property. The language of the imperial rescripts make it clear that they were considered a danger to public security because socially and intellectually divisive. It was inevitable that the imperial bureaucracy threw in its lot with those who stood for order and stability rather than individual initiative; and it was this which we now see blocked the development of a Christian lay culture in the Latin west. Even so, eighteen Italian bishops found themselves unable to conform and were removed from office; and Pelagianism remained a powerful element in the Gallic and British church. In those parts of the north-west provinces where the imperial writ ran intermittently if at all it survived strongly because most closely accommodating the situation on the ground. It was an heroic supposition that led the Gallic Chronicler to identify the year of Honorius' edict, 418, as 'the year in which Augustine is said to have invented the heresy of predestination'. The expeditions to Britain by the military bishop Germanus on behalf of the centralist party might rally large sections of the populace to organized national defence, but could not win the hearts and minds of those petty princelings that were the marked feature of the new age. Honorius had charged them to look to their own salvation, and that implied much more than merely the repeal of the *lex Iulii*; there could be no return. Constantius describes Germanus' confrontation with the Pelagian representative: a tyrannus—almost certainly Vortigern—surrounded by his *comites*, 'on the one side divine authority and on the other human presumption', their élitist and separatist views rejected by the rank and file. The Pelagian tyrannus would simply withdraw from the issue, allowing Germanus to take over temporary direction of military affairs. But the future lay with the new men; Vortigern recognized greater affinity with his Teutonic counterpart and would prefer to come to an understanding with men like Hengest. Elements in the insular church continued to be denounced abroad as 'Pelagian' as late as the seventh century. Certainly its adherents, British and Saxon, maintained a fiercely individualist spirit, deeply mistrusting centralism of any kind, scornful of the hierarchies of Mediterranean order and admitting no sacerdotal authority between the individual will and that of God. Aldhelm's letter to Geraint, a British prince in Devon, suggests that it was this temperamental and institutional issue, rather than the faintly ludicrous official agenda, which was the true conflict between the Roman and Celtic Churches at Whitby. Certainly it was this which led native princes to expel over-vigorous exponents of centralism like Wilfrid or Acca.

While the Pelagian ethic found its model in the heroic life, it was the centralist institution that generated and confirmed the feudalism to which European heroism would succumb. Ironically heroic society was doomed to extinction by the very fact of its success. The establishment of an imperium stretching beyond the confines of personal relationships requires that the comitatus dissolve in favour of a network of tenurial relationships, resulting in the death of the open society which was the breeding-ground of the heroic life. That the heroic spirit could persist strongly into the second half of the eighth century is proved by the story of Cynewulf and Cyneheard; and as a recognizable literary fiction it could be recalled as late as The Battle of Maldon. The heroic fact could scarcely survive the feudal ideology of Alcuin. In a sense, the last great heroes are the Mercian Æðelbald and the Austrasian Charles Martel. The failure of their respective hegemonies to survive marked the end of the European Heroic Age. Their successors would require a new and quite unheroic rationale to accommodate the new stability of western Europe: a new centralism of which Alcuin was the ideologue and which was institutionally embodied in the restoration of the Empire and a Roma Secunda at Aachen, which this time the attacks of other barbarians, Saracens from the south and Vikings from the north, would merely serve to confirm.

New battle literature could no longer ignore national and ethnic boundaries. Latter-day protagonists fight not for themselves but for larger concerns, an ethnic or religious cause and not merely their own: Roland or William *v*. Saracens, Alfred or Byrhtnoð *v*. Danes, Hereward *v*. Normans. The patriotic sentiment which leads Roland to speak of *France dulce* and William of Malmesbury to describe Edgar Ætheling as willing to lose all for the chance to live and die in England would have seemed inexplicable to their Migration Age forbears. Although they sometimes seem to strike the old heroic postures, and their exploits are indubitably valorous, theirs is not the individual heroic ideal that led Beowulf or Ingeld to their deaths. The restoration of confidence that the closed society brought muted and channelled notions of mutability into ready-made millennial beliefs like those portrayed in Wulfstan's *Sermo ad Anglos*. The literary materials of the Heroic Age which survived to be used anew, did so only in so far as they could be adapted to conform with the social truths of a later age—resulting in the strangely ambiguous world of the *Nibelungenlied*, while Arthur takes on a guise which Nennius could scarcely have recognized. When genuinely new war-literature emerges, it will present aspects of social realism on the one hand and authentic historical perspective on the other, represented by *Maldon* and *Brunanburh* respectively. Where heroic literature might have survived, in the free context of the Icelandic commonwealth, it entered a society with peasant rather than aristocratic concerns, and developed instead into the unique humanistic biography of the 'family-saga'.

Any reassessment of European heroic literature—so often equated simply with the literature of the Anglo-Saxon period as a whole—might usefully begin with an attempt to define its geographical and chronological boundaries with greater precision. And due recognition of the degree of homogeneity between contiguous European cultures might allow us to identify their diagnostic features with greater confidence. It is over sixty years ago that Sieper first demonstrated the relationship between the elegiac content of Old English and early Welsh poetry, and yet our university courses permit an original knowledge of both sources only to an occasional advanced student. The relevance of patristic studies to much of medieval literature is now well established, but the value of attempting to accommodate heroic literature to Mediterranean orthodoxies is questionable, while the area of greatest relevance, the seventy or so Pelagian tracts, remains as yet quite unexplored.

II

'That Shakespeherian Rag'

TERENCE HAWKES

'O, O, O, O'—not, you will be pleased to hear, the terminal hysteria of a cockney Santa Claus but, according to the Folio text, the last utterance of the Prince of Denmark. The rest there is not silence, but an expressive printer's signal, unanimously suppressed by editors as an 'actor's interpolation': an odd verdict, it might be concluded, on what might well rank as a perceptive gloss on the part by its first, and very astute critic, Richard Burbage.

Hamlet's death, after all, is a particular case of a man who has struggled mightily to win back for language something of its natural human authority, after that has been debased and debilitated by the actions of his 'mighty opposite' in the Danish court. That we should witness speech painfully and violently slain in him, hear his dying voice at last reduced to groaning, recognize in those O's how fearfully Claudius's poison denies him his just inheritance of silence, become revealing aspects of the play's statement. If this is interpolation, give us excess of it.

T. S. Eliot is not reckoned amongst the great Shakespearian critics. His failure with *Hamlet* has been seen as both notable and typical in that, as an American, he seems unable to grasp that play's links with a native, non-literary *English* tradition.[1] The mind that had 'never ... seen a cogent refutation of Thomas Rymer's objections to *Othello*' finds *Hamlet* 'most certainly an artistic failure' and ' ... full of some stuff that the writer could not drag to light, contemplate or manipulate into art'. Moreover, he admits that this 'feeling' is 'very difficult to localize. You cannot point to it in the speeches.' The essence of the play seems in fact to

[1] E.g. F. R. Leavis, *English Literature in Our Time and the University* (London, 1969), pp. 149–54.

lie 'beyond' the words which appear to embody it, in what he calls its 'unmistakable tone'.[1]

Recognition of 'tone' as an illuminating adjunct to the words is, as Christopher Ricks has recently argued, crucial to Eliot's own verse as it is to the whole Symbolist enterprise.[2] It is a quality residing perhaps (to use G. L. Trager's term)[3] in the 'paralinguistic' *voicing* of the words, over and above their overt meaning, that forms part of the oral dimension in which all plays deal. Constituting as it does a good deal of the ultimately achieved effect of Eliot's own verse, oral 'tone' becomes the element he responds most sensitively to in Shakespeare's.

Of course the word 'tone' also has a melodic dimension, aptly suggestive of the power of non-discursive musical sound to penetrate the heart and the brain. And the 'tonal' combination of words and music in popular song, together with the capacity of that combination literally to invade, to 'catch' our apprehensions and take them over, is intentionally hinted at in the title of this paper; a phrase that, however unlikely it may be to record the fact, nevertheless constitutes one of the most memorable links between two of the greatest poets in English: a wry 'tonal' acknowledgment perhaps, from the heart of a modern masterpiece, towards one of its author's own masters.

It would be uncharacteristic if it were not also fairly acute. And when we turn again to *The Waste Land*, it is to discover that at least one of the levels of irony implicit in that acknowledgment inheres in its knowing use of the same symbol of language tonally, orally conceived, that we have already encountered: 'O, O, O, O That Shakespeherian Rag'.

It will come as no surprise to those with a taste for Eliotic humour to learn that there really was such a song, as B. R.

---

[1] T. S. Eliot, *Selected Essays* (London, 1951), pp. 141–6.

[2] See the account of Christopher Ricks's unpublished lecture in *The Times Literary Supplement*, 2nd November 1973, p. 1345. Cf. the subsequent correspondence, pp. 1372, 1404, 1476, 1540 and 1589.

[3] G. L. Trager, 'Paralanguage: a first approximation', *Studies in Linguistics* Vol. 13, (1958), pp. 1–2. See also Trager's essay in Dell Hymes (ed.), *Language in Culture and Society* (New York, 1964), pp. 274–79.

McElderry has pointed out.[1] The work of the almost eponymous team of Gene Buck and Herman Ruby (words) and Dave Stamper (music), *That Shakespearian Rag*, with its chorus

> That Shakespearian Rag
> Most intelligent, very elegant,
> That old classical drag,
> Has the proper stuff, the line 'Lay on Macduff'

was one of the hit numbers of 1912, a year which offered it considerable competition in the shape of *Everybody's Doin' It* and *Be My Little Baby Bumble Bee*. Interestingly enough, its success was positively identified, in the advertisements promoting the song, with its oral performance. In *Variety* for October 25th of that year it was billed as 'Roy Samuels' big hit in *Ziegfeld's Follies of 1912*', and the song publishers, listing it fourth among ten titles in a *Variety* advertisement for July 19th of the same year, added: 'If you want a song that can be acted as well as sung send for this big surprise hit.' Eliot's 'interpolation' of the extra syllable in 'Shakespeherian', together with the O's, confirms and reinforces an oral dimension that obviously struck him as wholly appropriate (and indeed has turned out to be efficacious: line 128 of *The Waste Land* has preserved the song's banality far more effectively than the performance of Mr Samuels). The whole episode indicates a subtlety of ear, and a degree of oral-aural acuity that is distinctive.

It was an ear that recognized its own capabilities in Shakespeare. In a broadcast talk on John Dryden[2] in which Eliot compared parallel passages from *All For Love* and *Antony and Cleopatra* he had offered a precise instance. It concerns the death of Charmian.[3]

North's translation of Plutarch gives the following account of Charmian's last words:

[1] B. R. McElderry Jr, 'Eliot's "Shakespeherian Rag"', *American Quarterly*, Vol. 9 (1957), pp. 185–6.

[2] Published in *The Listener*, 22 April, 1931, pp. 681–2.

[3] Christopher Ricks makes exactly the point that follows, and in connection with the same material, in his review of volume VIII of Geoffrey Bullough's *Narrative and Dramatic Sources of Shakespeare* in *The Sunday Times*, 9 March, 1975.

One of the soldiers seeing her, angrily sayd unto her: Is that well done, Charmion? Verie well sayd she againe, and meet for a Princess descended from the race of so many noble kings.[1]

Dryden's version of this is:

> Yes, tis well done, and like a Queen, the last
> Of her great race: I follow her.
> *(Sinks down and dies)*
> (v. i)

Shakespeare's version is:

> It is well done, and fitting for a princess
> Descended of so many royal kings.

And then adds the two words:

> Ah, soldier!
> (v. ii. 326-8)

before she dies.

Eliot's comment on the difference between these versions indicates his perception of Shakespeare's remarkable sense of oral 'tone'. You cannot, he argues, 'say that the two lines of Dryden are either less poetic than Shakespeare's, or less dramatic'. The difference lies in the 'remarkable addition' to the original text of North: the 'two plain words, "Ah, soldier"'. Eliot finds himself nonplussed by the inexplicable effect of these words, for

> there is nothing in them for the actress to express in action; she can at best enunciate them clearly. I could not myself put into words the difference I feel between the passage if these two words, 'Ah, soldier', were omitted and with them. But I know there is a difference, and that only Shakespeare could have made it.[2]

---

[1] C. F. Tucker Brooke (ed.), *Shakespeare's Plutarch* (London, 1909), p. 193.
[2] Loc. cit., p. 681.

The difference is the more remarkable perhaps because of the deliberation with which it has been manufactured. North's Plutarch is both explicit and emphatic in ending Charmian's words where Dryden leaves them, even adding:

> She sayd no more; but fell down
> dead hard by the bed.

What Shakespeare adds, what Eliot discerns and finds himself inexplicably respondent to, are two words that signal a whole world of expressive bodily movement that must lie beyond the words themselves. It is nonsense of course to say that there is nothing in these words that can be expressed in action: nonsense because that denies the fundamental relationship of words to action that *Antony and Cleopatra* has been at pains fully to explore.

In fact, it may be argued that nobody just talks; that communication properly requires a complex and interdependent relationship between voice and body, sound and gesture.[1] *Antony and Cleopatra* is a play about two flawed worlds in which that necessary, humanizing interdependency has ceased to operate. Voice alone dominates the Roman world; body alone that of Egypt. Rome is a place of words, Egypt a place of actions. Rome is where love is talked of, Egypt is where love is made.

Antony accordingly finds himself committed and limited— albeit willingly—to a way of life in which the body rules the voice. And his commitment finds itself unerringly signalled in the play's first scene, by an appropriately wordless gesture. 'Kingdoms are clay' he pronounces,

> . . . the nobleness of life
> Is to do thus.
>
> (I. i. 35–7)

whereupon he turns and kisses Cleopatra.

The importance of this gesture to the play's theme can be judged from the risk it evidently takes of embarrassing or distracting an

---

[1] See my arguments in *Shakespeare's Talking Animals* (London, 1973), pp. 15–23 and 178–91.

audience aware that women's parts are played by boy actors. Like most contemporary dramatists, Shakespeare rarely permits much physical contact on stage between men and 'women' for this reason. The memorable reference on Cleopatra's part to the fact that her own greatness might be 'boyed' in the Roman streets (v. ii. 220–1), together with other frequent reminders that 'she' is a boy, serve to focus an 'alienated' and thus powerfully reiterated attention on this physical aspect of her relationship with Antony throughout the play.

In short, that moment when their bodies unite on the stage turns out to be paradigmatic. The word 'thus', and its accompanying gesture, signals a totally physical way of life committed to communication primarily through and with the body. The beds in the east are soft. There, the intensest kind of wordless bodily communion prevails. Antony's blush (i. i. 30) 'speaks' volumes. Hands, not words, are 'read'. Close physical, tactile contact constitutes the mode of everyday existence, and in performance the spatial relationship between the actors' bodies must be a good deal closer in the Egyptian scenes than in those set in Rome. Cleopatra's own person proves word-defeating: it beggars all descriptions, and both she and her attendants tend to use language itself less as a vehicle for rational discourse than as a physically luxurious entity. Even a surprised messenger is likely to find himself urged alarmingly to

> Ram thou thy fruitful tidings in mine ears
> That long time have been barren.
> (ii. v. 23—4)

In this context Antony's death presents itself in appropriately sensual, sexual terms: he resolves to be

> A bridegroom in my death, and run into't
> As to a lover's bed.
> (iv. xiv. 100–1)

And he ends in that vein by falling on his sword claiming, to the aptly named Eros, that

> ... To do thus
> I learned of thee.
> (102–3)

Of course there is an apt pun on 'death' (in the sense of sexual climax) which the play exploits at length both here and throughout. In a world where the 'nobleness of life' resides in 'doing thus' with such frequency, Enobarbus's commentary on Cleopatra's 'celerity in dying'—her response to the 'mettle in death' (I. ii. 143ff.)—has a double edge. It is wholly appropriate, then, that at the play's end she should speak of 'immortal longings' in her own body, discover that

> The stroke of death is as a lover's pinch
> Which hurts and is desired.
> (v. ii. 295–6)

and so generate the pun's final explicit irony. A life based on 'doing thus' as its sole end finds nothing at its conclusion but a grimmer and more final version of the 'death' it has punningly pursued all along. Cleopatra's physical death is the fitting 'climax' of her many sexual 'deaths'. Induced by the fondled, phallic asp, it has, properly, an orgasmic dimension, overt, yet beyond the words:

> As sweet as balm, as soft as air, as gentle –
> O Antony! ...
> (v. ii. 311–12)

And when Charmian dies, shortly afterwards, that body-dominated world of 'doing thus' finally dies—in every sense—with her. For her 'Ah Soldier'—matching her mistress's 'O, Antony'—signals, indeed *is*, its death-knell, and it bespeaks an appropriate and orgasmic last gesture from the boy actor, fully suggestive of the pun on death, by whose means the uncomprehending Roman soldier, and the world of mere words he represents, is wordlessly mocked.

King Lear's reductive insistence upon explicit statement, and its analogue in the realm of knowledge, quantity and calculation, indicates by comparison a way of life utterly unable to cope with the wordless. It accordingly regards silence, and so, concomitantly, gesture, as uncommunicative. Cordelia's awareness that her love is more ponderous than her tongue, that she cannot 'heave/My heart into my mouth', her resolve to 'Love and be silent' in the face of her sisters' facile wordiness are thus fated to meet only incomprehension.

As Jill Levenson has pointed out, the play insists on the point.[1] Cordelia's silence is Shakespeare's own addition to the story. Its purpose is to demonstrate the limitations Lear imposes on language by his insistence on words alone as the carriers of meaning. And, in the division scene, we see him deceived by words alone; particularly by a sophistication of the word 'love' itself which, in its punning dimension of 'assess the price or value of something' has a central subversive function.[2] Lear's simplistic misconception of that word's manifold dimensions finally draws from him the tragically reductive equation by whose lights his own punishment is ultimately calculated: 'Nothing will come of nothing'. Only a mind which links 'something' inextricably with measurable verbal protestation could respond in such a limited fashion to the reality each of his daughters manifests *in propria persona*.

We have noted the central pun on 'death' in *Antony and Cleopatra*, and the pun on 'love' in *King Lear* has no less crucial a function. In fact it would be salutary to remind ourselves at this point that it is only a highly literate society that judges the pun to be the lowest form of wit. In a community dependent upon the *sound* of the human voice and the physical presence of the body which, gesturally, can indicate the homonym, the pun enjoys considerable status. Because it draws upon the totality of communicative processes, and because, glorying in these, it literally is enabled to go 'beyond' the simple word that generates it, the pun seems to embody almost the essence of the spoken language.

---

[1] Jill Levenson, 'What the Silence said: Still points in *King Lear*' in Clifford Leech and J. M. R. Margeson (eds.), *Shakespeare 1971: Proceedings of the World Shakespeare Congress* (Toronto, 1972), pp. 215–29.
[2] See *Shakespeare's Talking Animals*, cit., pp. 167–72.

The potential Elizabethan pun on 'nothing' seems to represent almost an affirmation of that society's orality because its homonym 'noting' refers of course precisely to that perceptive act to which non-verbal communication—literally without words—appeals. In Lear's case, what is clearly at stake in the 'nothing/noting' homonym is the question of looking beyond mere words to the 'silence' that Cordelia indicates best expresses her love. Were Lear to 'note' that, embodied as it is in her physical bearing, he would indeed 'see better'.

The body, after all, talks. And the nature of human communication requires, as I have said, that we 'note' its language as adjunctive to and moderative of what the voice says. This, to use the modern term, 'kinesic' dimension receives its clearest definition perhaps in that play of Shakespeare's whose title embodies this very pun.

In *Much Ado About Nothing*, 'noting' does indeed stand for the silent dimension of the speech-act: the 'nothing' which must be added as a redeeming, validating agent to the 'something' of verbal protestation. The inability to 'note' beyond the level of mere words pervades the entire society of Messina. So, when Claudio falsely accuses Hero, only the Friar, who alone has 'noted' her correctly, can save her from disgrace and death.[1] He breaks his own silence to make the point:

> Hear me a little;
> For I have only been silent so long,
> And given way unto this course of fortune
> By noting of the lady. I have marked
> A thousand blushing apparitions
> To start into her face, a thousand innocent shames
> In angel whiteness beat away those blushes;
> And in her eye there hath appeared a fire,
> To burn the errors that these Princes hold
> Against her maiden truth.
>
> (IV. i. 153–62)

[1] This point is brilliantly made by David Horowitz in *Shakespeare, an Existential View* (London, 1965), pp. 19-21.

When Lear enters, finally, with Cordelia dead in his arms, we find him very obviously having outrun the same limits of verbal protestation. As he throws back his head and howls, linguistic 'something' offers no forms adequate for his situation:

> Howl, howl, howl, howl! O you are men of stones!
> Had I your tongues and eyes I'd use them so
> That heaven's vault should crack . . .
> (v. iii. 259–61)

He looks beyond language, for breath to 'mist or stain' a glass, for a feather to stir as evidence of life, not words. Indeed, the absence of words, and Cordelia's involvement with silence, her long-standing commitment to the non-verbal, is stressed; together with the newly urgent sense that her 'nothing' now—as always—communicates:

> Cordelia, Cordelia, stay a little. Ha,
> What is't thou say'st? Her voice was ever soft,
> Gentle and low, an excellent thing in woman.
> (v. iii. 273–5)

Critics have differed about the import of Lear's last words, but their direction seems clear. It is towards 'noting', away from 'nothing'.

The reference to the hanging of his 'poor fool' (v. iii. 308) links the two thematically related functions performed by the body of the boy actor (who has perhaps also played both parts) and draws attention to that body lying now in his arms. The repeated 'Never, never, never, never, never' (l. 310) teeters on the edge of speech, virtually committing itself to a dimension of pure, non-discursive sound (Eliot himself termed the line 'sounding', meaning 'musical'). And then, as music does, the play wordlessly draws from us the necessary final, completing response.

The body of the boy actor is exhibited. 'Pray you undo this button' (l.311) represents, surely, Lear's request for Edgar or Kent to undo a button on the boy actor's costume. This done, after the phatic 'Thank you sir' there follows in the Pide Bull

Quarto the wordless 'O, O, O, O' that we have 'noted' before. The boy actor's head, perhaps because the button was restraining it, now lolls back, possibly revealing, also wordlessly, the damage to the larynx wrought by the hanging noose. And then Lear directs our attention with even greater intensity—'Do you see this? Look on her'—to the organs of speech themselves:

> Look, her lips,
> Look there, look there!
> (v. iii. 312–13)

Surely, Cordelia's mouth falls open. Perhaps the lips, in their deathly *rigor*, seem even to frame words. But the silence that comes from them weighs far more heavily than words ever could. In death, as in life, she speaks without words: says everything by saying—literally at last—'nothing'. And Lear dies finally, tragically, 'noting' the wordless eloquence in which her 'nothing' consists.

He invites us to do the same. To 'note' the oral, non-discursive, *performed* dimensions of the play that lie beyond the words, animate, and ultimately transcend them. At the furthest reach of the pun on 'noting' (*via* 'notation') it is 'tonal', it is 'musical', it is 'sound' advice.

The recent revival of interest in classical ragtime music has placed it in quite a different perspective from that encouraged by the word 'ragtime' and its users in the years following the first world war, when an attempt was made to link it with the emergent, challenging music of black America in the form of the blues and jazz. In fact, ragtime represents a quite different, opposite mode. It is an essentially *written* music, to be played (the classical ragtime composers insist on this) *as written* on the piano. Its import is fundamentally opposed to that of the blues and jazz, in that it represents a 'writing-down' of the *orality* which blues and jazz promote. Its whole bearing is the reverse of the black and the improvisatory. It constitutes a bid on the part of its early (and best) exponents for genteel, white, European respectability. Its aim is to be both 'elegant' and 'intelligent', and the monuments to this endeavour are the black ragtime composer Scott Joplin's (1868–1917) two ill-fated ragtime operas *A Guest of Honour* (1903) and *Treemonisha* (1911).

After Sedalia, Missouri, whose Maple Leaf Café is commemorated in Joplin's enormously popular *Maple Leaf Rag* (1899), the great formative centre of ragtime was St Louis. Joplin himself moved there in 1900; the lost *A Guest of Honour* achieved its single recorded performance there in 1903. And in 1904 the city was host to a National Ragtime Contest. Moreover, St Louis was, and is, not unknown for its connection with the great native American art—ragtime's opposite—the Blues. Anyone with any connection with St Louis in those years (and Eliot's was close enough for him to make an unwarranted, but clearly deeply felt and embarrassing reference in later years to his own oral relationship with the city— his 'nigger drawl')[1] would have heard in the air—could hardly have avoided 'noting'—the opposed polarities of native American music: on the one hand 'written' ragtime, on the other the 'orality' of blues and jazz that ragtime specifically denied.

On another level, such a polarization could be said to be of a fundamental order. It represents perhaps, in miniature, an unresolvable dichotomy that, experienced as indicative of a deeper rift, and raised to a higher symbolic power, might ultimately lay waste any culture: deny it, in terms of Eliot's later vision, the cohesion whose absence *The Waste Land* and much of his critical enterprise laments.

Ironically, the presumed embodiment of that presupposed cohesion, the plays of Shakespeare, have found themselves over the centuries forced into the service of the same cultural dichotomy. Beginning as the high peak of the English-speaking culture's *popular* art, they have over 400 years dwindled to become the exemplars of an exclusive high art. From their function as the demotic, oral externalization of the totality of their own culture, they have shrunk to be sacred written texts; their guardians, from Dr Johnson on, ever eager to expunge from their pages the

---

[1] Quoted by Herbert Read in Allen Tate (ed.), *T. S. Eliot: the Man and His Work* (London, 1967), p. 15.

betraying signs of orality. 'A dramatic exhibition', Johnson thunders, in his *Preface to the Plays of William Shakespeare* (1765), 'is a book recited with concomitants that increase or diminish its effect'. If 'Familiar comedy is often more powerful on the theatre than in the page; imperial tragedy is always less . . . A play read affects the mind like a play acted'.

It is worth checking our risibility for the moment to reflect that the Johnsonian voice, ever ready to excise or 'blot' from Shakespeare's 'book' such 'forced and unnatural metaphors' as may fail, *inter alia*, to match the requirements of *written* sense, still makes itself heard in the land. Terms as confident in their presuppositions as 'intrusive matter', 'actors' interpolations', 'stage accretions' deriving from 'corruption through performance' remain the common coin of one kind of Shakespearian criticism.[1]

But 'intrusive' *into* what? 'accretions' *onto* what? 'corruptions' *of* what? There is no pristine manuscript of any of Shakespeare's plays. And if there were, on what basis would we grant it stronger authority, say, than the text of a prompt-book which relates, with some immediacy, to an actual contemporary performance in which the author's acquiescence was not improbable?[2] Those who, seeking to make the plays 'elegant' and 'intelligent', speak slightingly of 'actors' interpolations' in them should remember that Shakespeare himself was an actor.

We are dealing, after all, with constructs that are made out of and, as I have argued elsewhere, can be said to be substantially *about*, speech.[3] And speech has, in drama as in life, a primarily oral-aural bearing. It thus appeals beyond the visual level of the imagination, to a level which Eliot himself described as 'auditory':

. . . the feeling for syllable and rhythm, penetrating far below the conscious levels of thought and feeling, invigorating every word; sinking to the most primitive and forgotten, returning

---

[1] See Harold Jenkins, 'Playhouse Interpolations in the Folio text of *Hamlet*', *Studies in Bibliography*, XIII, 1960, pp. 31–47.

[2] Cf. Jenkins, 'An editor who thought so might have a pretty problem on his hands'.

[3] *Shakespeare's Talking Animals*, cit., pp. 24–30.

to the origin and bringing something back, seeking the beginning and the end. It works through meanings, certainly, or not without meanings in the ordinary sense, and fuses the old and obliterated and the trite, the current, and the new and surprising, the most ancient and the most civilized mentality.[1]

It is a level where the Johnsonian *dicta* prove inadequate to the complexities generated by the multi-dimensional nature of Shakespeare's oral-aural art, with its sense of simultaneity effortlessly maintained between separately articulated levels of meaning.

Indeed, if we agree with Claude Lévi-Strauss that 'impoverishment and mutilation' is the inevitable lot of orality reduced to the level of the written word, then the model of the play's own orality, of what (in the aptly named 'Overture' to *The Raw And The Cooked*) he calls the 'language which transcends the level of articulated language', must obviously and more precisely be located elsewhere.[2]

The link between drama and music lies of course in the element of performance. And no reader of Eliot can fail to feel at home with Lévi-Strauss's account of the process: 'In listening to music—and while we are listening—we have achieved a kind of immortality ... The music lives out its life in me; I listen to myself through the music'.[3] In Eliot's words (from the *Four Quartets*) this becomes:

> ... music heard so deeply
> That it is not heard at all, but you are the music
> While the music lasts.
>
> (*The Dry Salvages*)

The sense of 'being' the performance is of course crucial to audiences of both music and drama. It is the response that validates

---

[1] *The Use of Poetry and the Use of Criticism*, 1933.
[2] Claude Lévi-Strauss, *The Raw and the Cooked* (*Le Cru et le Cuit*), trans. John and Doreen Weightman (London, 1970).
[3] Ibid.

and makes viable the act of 'playing'. Music works by literally involving itself with the 'organic rhythms' of our bodies. Its rhythms connect with, invite a participatory response from, and finally invade and take over the rhythms of our cardiac and respiratory systems. This is how the performance of 'popular' melodies 'catches' us; it is how Eliot's own symbolist verse works, invading the mind, penetrating 'below the conscious levels of thought and feeling'.

And indeed the essence of that native American musical tradition, ragtime's opposite—blues and jazz, lies in exactly this process: in its involving orality, the identity it insistently demands of audience and performance, and of performance and performer; a performance whose 'interpolations' in and onto the original sequence of chords literally *constitute* the music, and make the player, what he plays, and his audience, simultaneously part of the same momentary whole.

In an oral society, an actor's 'playing' will involve the same process, invite the same implicating response. And in the form of qualities which cannot be 'dragged to light', which you cannot 'point to in the speeches', but which, as in 'O, O, O, O' or 'Ah Soldier', or Cordelia's mute body, exhibit an involving, identifying *musical* power *beyond* that of mere words, this is the fundamental 'oral' feature that Eliot was perceptive enough to 'note' as 'unmistakable' in Shakespeare's plays. In fact Eliot's continuing interest in popular and 'performed' oral culture needs little demonstration. The typescript of the early draft of *The Waste Land* shows a distinctive oral bearing. It is full of voices (the first part of the poem in this version is entitled *He Do The Police In Different Voices*)—and these are memorably demotic.[1] It is also, as we have noted, strewn with snatches of popular songs. And it is hardly surprising that when Eliot transferred himself to England, this interest persisted in the form of his frequenting Edwardian music-halls.

He was, of course, not thinking specifically of Shakespeare when, writing of the 'moral superiority' of the greatest British

---

[1] Valerie Eliot (ed.), *The Waste Land; A Facsimile and Transcript of the Original Draft* (London, 1971), pp. 4ff.

music-hall star of her day, he pointed out, with little trace of distorting American presupposition, that

> The working man who went to the music-hall and saw Marie Lloyd, and joined in the chorus, was himself performing part of the act; he was engaged in that collaboration of the audience with the artist which is necessary in all art and most obviously in dramatic art.[1]

But that creative 'collaboration' clearly constitutes a good deal of what may be termed the genuine Shakespearian 'music'—truly elegant, truly intelligent—demeaned by the exploitative vulgarity (and, incidentally, wholly mistaken musical assumptions) of Messrs Buck, Ruby and Stamper's *Shakespearian Rag*.

Perhaps only Coleridge has put it better. Speaking of Shakespeare he says: 'You feel him to be a poet inasmuch as for a time he has made you one—an active, creative being'.[2] In short, like all oral art that is *genuinely* popular (as the blues was, as Marie Lloyd's was), Shakespeare's plays—the Shakespe*her*ian Rag—reach out to us (as it were, with that extra, paralinguistic syllable), invade us and invite us to make (with that 'O, O, O, O') a sympathetic—an acoustic—act of 'closure' with themselves. Properly 'noted', as the groaning Burbage knew, they thereby turn us from spectators into participants.

One final point. An art committed to oral, involving performance is committed, by the same token, to ephemerality. Drama is permanent. But individual plays must be as ephemeral as individual performances of them.

Far from proving exceptions to this rule, Shakespeare's plays exemplify it. Events at any of our contemporary Stratfords unwittingly reveal far more about our own world's preoccupations than about Shakespeare's. Ephemerality will out.

Perhaps the full implication of *The Shakespeherian Rag* lies in the fact that it is, quite simply, 'dated'. And 'dating' bespeaks,

---

[1] *Selected Essays*, cit., p. 458.
[2] Terence Hawkes (ed.), *Coleridge on Shakespeare* (Penguin Books, Harmondsworth, 1969), p. 65.

literally, a commitment to immediacy, and so a release from posterity's crippling embrace. Who now frets to establish the 'true text' of the *Ziegfeld Follies of 1912*? The presence of 'interpolations' into (my own favourite) *Naughty Girls of 1947* wrings few withers. As clearly 'dated' popular art, these inherit the ephemerality which their nature makes their right.

When Burbage died, a contemporary elegy claimed the same right in respect of *his* work:

> No more young Hamlett, ould Heironymoe
> Kind Leer, the greued Moore, and more beside,
> That liued in him, haue now for ever dyde.[1]

Let his true monument then, and that of the parts that lived in him, be those poignant wordless sounds with which I began: O, O, O, O. They represent, orally, a language (as well as, visually, a theatre) which—beyond mere words—was able to generate the quintessence of drama. As Burbage himself, Shakespeare, and the American Eliot knew, that makes them *verba sapienti* every one.

[1] The elegy is ascribed to 'Jo ffletcher'. See C. C. Stopes, *Burbage and Shakespeare's Stage* (London, 1913).

III

The Statue of Hermione

TERENCE SPENCER

To begin with, there is a logical difficulty in talking about Hermione's statue in *The Winter's Tale*. For, of course, there isn't a statue at all, and never has been. We in the audience are given information which arouses our curiosity, holds us in suspense, and prepares us for the surprise of seeing the boy actor standing very still in a statuesque posture in the last scene of the play: *Enter Leontes, Polixenes, Florizell, Perdita, Camillo, Paulina; Hermione (like a Statue:) Lords, &c.*

We first hear about this supposed miracle of art from an anonymous Third Gentleman, who had, however, on entry been identified as 'the Lady *Paulina*'s Steward' (v. ii. 26). The princess Perdita 'with all greedinesse of affection' is going to visit 'her Mothers Statue (which is in the keeping of *Paulina*)'. It is said to be 'a Peece many yeeres in doing, and now newly perform'd, by that rare Italian Master, *Iulio Romano*'. Then follows the praise of the master's powers of realistic portrayal of Nature and, in particular, of this statue of Hermione: he is an artist

> who (had he himselfe Eternitie, and could put Breath into his Worke) would beguile Nature of her Custome, so perfectly he is her Ape; He so neere to *Hermione*, hath done *Hermione*, that they say one would speake to her, and stand in hope of answer.

If submitted to rational analysis this part of the plot is deplorable: the emphatic and plausible ascription of the statue to a famous sculptor is superfluous and (if we were capable of giving our full attention in the theatre) inconvenient. We are told that a well-known artist (he is *that* rare Italian master) has been for many years engaged on a posthumous statue, and presumably for that purpose resident meanwhile in or near Paulina's 'removed House'; and that many people have seen the statue in 'the Chappell' there and admired its realistic presentment of the long-dead Queen. It is yet another example of Shakespeare's theatrical legerdemain. He had to prepare for the *coup de théâtre* in the next scene (v. iii), which was to be something novel and audacious: a Galatea-like, on-stage transformation of a supposed statue into a human being. What is worth investigating is why he chose the words he did in order to stimulate our curiosity and carry conviction. Why *Julio Romano*? Why an *Italian* master? And why the particular details which emphasize the realistic technique of the statue?

Leontes   . . .we came
   To see the Statue of our Queene. Your Gallerie
   Have we pass'd through, not without much content
   In many singularities; but we saw not
   That which my Daughter came to looke upon,
   The Statue of her Mother.
Paulina   . . .here it is: prepare
   To see the Life as lively mock'd, as ever
   Still Sleepe mock'd Death . . .
Leontes   Her naturall Posture.
   Chide me (deare Stone) that I may say indeed
   Thou art *Hermione* . . . But yet (*Paulina*)
   Hermione was not so much wrinckled, nothing
   So aged as this seemes . . .
Paulina   So much the more our Carvers excellence,
   Which lets goe-by some sixteene yeeres, and makes her
   As she liv'd now.
Leontes   . . . . Oh, thus she stood,
   Even with such Life of Maiestie (warme Life,
   As now it coldly stands) when first I woo'd her.
   . . . Oh Royall Peece . . .
Perdita   And give me leave,
   And doe not say tis Superstition, that
   I kneele, and then implore her Blessing. Lady,
   Deere Queene, that ended when I but began,
   Give me that hand of yours, to kisse.

Paulina O, patience:
  The Statue is but newly fix'd; the Colour's
  Not dry . . .
Leontes Doe not draw the Curtaine.
Paulina No longer shall you gaze on't, least your Fancie
  May thinke anon, it moves.
Leontes Let be, let be:
  Would I were dead, but that me thinkes alreadie.
  (What was he that did make it?) See (my Lord)
  Would you not deeme it breath'd? and that those veines
  Did verily beare blood?
Polixenes Masterly done:
  The very Life seemes warme upon her Lippe.
Leontes The fixure of her Eye ha's motion in't,
  As we are mock'd with Art.
                    . . . . Let no man mock me,
  For I will kisse her.
Paulina Good my Lord, forbeare:
  The ruddinesse upon her Lippe, is wet:
  You'le marre it, if you kisse it; stayne your owne
  With Oyly Painting: shall I draw the Curtaine.
Leontes No: not these twentie yeeres . . .
Paulina Either forbeare,
  Quit presently the Chappell, or resolve you
  For more amazement.

In the first place, the name 'Julio Romano' is, we must agree, a
perfect one for theatrical enunciation in the situation. Replace him
for a moment by one of the real Italian sculptors of the time
(Dionigi Bussola, Giovanni d'Enrico, Cristoforo Prestinari,
Giovanni Tabachetti, Melchiorre Righi), and we at once see how
much plausibility lay in Shakespeare's choice. But the appearance
of 'Julio Romano' here has aroused a good deal of comment.
Editors from the eighteenth century onwards have taken this to be
a reference to Giulio Pippi (1499–1546), commonly called
Giulio Romano from his birthplace—a famous pupil of Raphael.
He was, however, a painter and architect. No sculptural works by
him are known or recorded. So, it was decided, Shakespeare is not

only being 'anachronistic' but also 'inaccurate' in using this name as the 'performer' of Hermione's statue.

Some efforts have of course been made to exonerate Shakespeare from the charge of carelessness or ignorance. It has been pointed out that there are statues occasionally in the backgrounds of Giulio Romano's pictures; perhaps this led to Shakespeare's confusion? Moreover Giulio Romano's epitaph in the church of St Barnaba in Mantua (recorded by Vasari in the first edition of his *Lives* in 1550) seems to refer to sculpture as well as painting:

> Videbat Juppiter corpora sculpta pictaque
> spirare, et aedes mortalium aequarier Caelo
> Julii virtute Romani.

But it is a rather far-fetched idea to suppose that Shakespeare was misled by this epitaph. Perhaps Shakespeare, it may be added, was impressed by the well-known versatility of Italian artists and imagined that one of those masters could turn his hand with equal success to any of the arts.

This may be the clue we need. No doubt Giulio Romano, the painter and architect, was the best-known person of that name in the eighteenth and nineteenth centuries, and still is so. But was this true at the time when Shakespeare was writing *The Winter's Tale*? Guilio Romano had died as long ago as 1546. Allusions to him in English writings are not numerous. Ben Jonson drops his name among the artists with whose works he would, ironically, furnish the house of the Lord Treasurer of England:

> I would, if price, or prayer could them get,
>   Send in, what or *Romano, Tintoret,*
> *Titian,* or *Raphael, Michael Angelo,*
>   Have left in fame to equall, or out-goe
> The old Greek-hands in picture, or in stone.
>   (*Underwoods,* LXXVII)

Perhaps Giulio Romano was best known, alas, as the originator of the obscene drawings of 'postures' which, engraved by Marcantonio Raimondi in 1524, were for long in circulation with explanatory sonnets by Aretino. (But I forbear from suggesting—

though it seems fashionable to descry irrelevant bawdy in Shakespeare—that Giulio's name here is an appalling jest for the benefit of the *cognoscenti*, who would snigger again at the allusion to Hermione's 'naturall Posture' in v. iii. 23.)

The unanimous linking of the sculptor of Hermione's statue with Giulio Pippi may have been too hasty. There were other 'rare Italian masters' called Giulio Romano. Not a sculptor, as far as I know, but there were two musicians. One of them is obscure, though a contemporary of Shakespeare. The other was far from obscure. Giulio Caccini (*c.* 1545–1618), called from his birthplace Giulio Romano, was a musician who played an important part in establishing and spreading throughout Europe new modes of Italian music. His madrigals in *Le nuove Musiche* (Venice, 1602), with an important critical preface, showed his new manner and were widely disseminated. It was (to quote Grove's *Dictionary of Music and Musicians*) 'an epoch-making work, the announcement to the world, though not the origin, of the new style of music known as monody'.

We can even guess the place where the name of *this* Giulio Romano had recently caught Shakespeare's eye. In 1610, shortly before the writing of *The Winter's Tale*, Robert Dowland published *A Musicall Banquet. Furnished with varietie of delicious Ayres, Collected out of the best Authors in English, French, Spanish and Italian*. This collection of lute songs was, as Dowland frankly acknowledged in his preface 'To the Reader', gathered from the works of 'the rarest and most judicious Maisters' in several countries of Europe (compare 'that rare Italian Master'). At the heading of both nos. XVIII and XIX appears the attribution '*Giulio Caccini detto Romano*'. As the name is also given above the 'Basso' part, it appears four times on consecutive pages.

The existence of other Giulio Romanos besides Giulio Pippi should confirm our belief that Shakespeare knew that this was an excellent generalized name for an Italian artist, however vague his memories may have been regarding particular individuals of that name.

Why the emphasis on the rare *Italian* artist? Why should this seem to be theatrically effective? Perhaps Shakespeare (and some of his audience) had heard something about contemporary sculpture in Italy which would give point to the allusion.

The Winter's Tale is not a play in which geography can be regarded as an organizing principle. The sea coast of Bohemia, with its harbour from which Prince Florizel sets sail for Sicilia with his party, has been a jest since Ben Jonson's day. The isle of Delphos, where the oracle of Apollo may be consulted, has been condemned (rather unfairly) as careless. And at one moment in the play Queen Hermione astounds the audience by the statement: 'The Emperor of Russia was my Father'—which stretched even the talents of Mary Cowden Clarke to explain away. At Leontes's court we are in Sicilia, which by Shakespeare might have been regarded as within the 'geographical expression', Italy. Yet 'that rare Italian Master' who carved the alleged statue sounds like a foreigner. As in his allusions to Whitsun pastorals and to Puritans who sing psalms to hornpipes, Shakespeare is momentarily back in England, where an Italian artist of distinction (like Federico Zuccari) might still occasionally appear. After all, the statue might well have been attributed to an English-born sculptor. 'That rare British master, Gerard Johnson' would do (if the Dutch form of his name, Gheerart Janssen, was too uncouth for the stage); and it would have been a nice compliment to the sculptor of Shakespeare's own future monumental bust in the chancel of Holy Trinity Church in Stratford-upon-Avon. Certainly Shakespeare had observed a good many funerary statues in churches. Iachimo exclaims in Imogen's bedchamber:

> O sleepe, thou Ape of death, lye dull upon her,
> And be her Sense but as a Monument,
> Thus in a Chappel lying.
>
> *(Cymbeline* II. ii. 31)

And Shakespeare knew the difference between good and bad workmanship in the plastic arts:

> a Stone-cutter, or a Painter, could not have made him so ill, though they had bin but two yeares oth' trade

is Kent's opinion of Oswald (*King Lear* II. ii. 62). In the churches of London and throughout England were many charming funerary statues, lying supine or kneeling in prayer. It must be admitted, however, that they were not of such realism that one would speak to them and stand in hope of answer.

Many of Shakespeare's comedies and tragedies have an Italianate setting, and this justified a certain amount of 'local colour'. Nightingales sing on pomegranate trees in Verona. The journey from the mainland over to Venice is by means of the traject or common ferry; there one hears news on the Rialto and meets a friend at lodgings in the Sagittary. It is possible that before writing *Othello* Shakespeare read Lewis Lewkenor's *The Commonwealth and Government of Venice* (1599), but it is equally possible that he had learned what he needed for his play from conversation with someone who had been to Venice and perhaps read on the spot the booklet by Gasparo Contarini which Lewkenor had translated. But the record of impressions of visitors to Italy in Shakespeare's lifetime is tantalizingly meagre. Discussions of the educational value of travel were tediously numerous; but what did these men *feel* when they walked among the glories of the Italian High Renaissance? All they could produce for us are the compilations of Fynes Moryson and the eccentricities of Tom Coryat and William Lithgow. It is an exciting moment when we read in one of Sir Philip Sidney's letters that there are two well-respected painters in Venice nowadays, Tintoretto and Paolo Veronese, and that he has chosen to have his portrait painted by the latter.

We all have fond memories of our first impressions of Italy; and so likewise did Shakespeare's contemporaries. But during the last few generations visitors have usually arrived by railway in Milan, Genoa, or Florence; and nowadays the bus awaits at the airport near Pisa or Rome to give newcomers their first impressions. In earlier centuries it was different. The sea route from Marseilles to Genoa excused one from the horrors of the Alps, but was often interrupted by fear of plague or pirates. Those who braved the Alpine passes had their rewards. From the difficulties of the pre-Napoleonic Simplon, for example, one dropped down to the pretty little town of Domo d'Ossola, otherwise Domodossola, in its Italianate landscape and (usually) Italianate weather. But neither Domodossola nor the next town on the route, Omegna, were likely to detain travellers for long by their productions of the Italian artistic genius. But at Orta, 29 miles further on, things were different.

Here—and in Varallo, Varesse, Oropo, Crea, and elsewhere—in Shakespeare's lifetime, began one of the extraordinary manifestations of late sixteenth-century Italian artistic enterprise, largely inspired by Carlo and Federico Borromeo. A series of hillside shrines or chapels were built from the 1590s onwards, containing intensely realistic, life-size sculptural scenes of religious subjects. The terra-cotta figures are not only naturalistically coloured, but often draped with appropriate clothing and embellished with human hair and glass eyes. Each chapel is enclosed, but through a small wire grating in front the interior scene is visible from the point of view and perspective intended by the designer. The effect is startling. Even today, when many of the chapels have become decayed and faded, it is an unforgettable experience to peer through the gratings at these vividly-realized scenes. We can guess what it was like when the statues were fresh from the artists' hands, newly painted, carefully lit. Varallo, probably the earliest, has forty-four chapels with scenes from the life of Christ. At Orta, begun in 1592, there are eighteen, representing the life of St Francis, and this gave scope for many lively episodes. At Varese, initiated in 1604, are fifteen scenes of the life of the Virgin. The first chapel, the Annunciation (dated 1609), is particularly astonishing as one gazes inside. For the Virgin stands beside her bed in a fully furnished room, her slippers being neatly tucked under the bed. Similarly, at Oropo there are seventeen chapels and at Crea (begun in 1589) twenty-three.

For a long time now these extraordinary works of sculpture have received scant attention from the guide books (except the local ones for the benefit of pilgrims). The authors of the classic books about travel in this part of Italy had little patience when confronted with such artistic appeals to their emotions. S. W. King in *The Italian Valleys of the Pennine Alps* (1858), while warmly commending the works of the painter Gaudenzio Ferrari and admitting that some of the sculptural groups had great merit, said that others were 'very inferior and mere rubbish' (chapter XX). Richard Bagot in *The Lakes of Northern Italy* (1907), was offended by the 'painful realism' of the Lombard artists (chapter XII) and dismisses

> the usual painful and sometimes revolting representations of the different episodes of the Crucifixion, or other subjects of a similar disagreeable and unedifying nature.
>
> (chapter XV)

Only Samuel Butler in his delightful *Alps and Sanctuaries* (1881) eccentrically and justly appreciated their merits, explaining that

> the desire was to bring the whole scene more vividly before the faithful by combining the picture, the statue, and the effect of a scene upon the stage in a single work of art.
>
> (chapter XV)

Then, as now, no one was allowed to enter the chapels, except to undertake repairs. It is a great surprise to see a living figure among the statues. As Butler amusingly explained:

> If the living figure does not move much, it is easy at first to mistake it for a terra-cotta one. At Orta, some years since, looking one evening into a chapel when the light was fading, I was surprised to see a saint whom I had not seen before; he had no glory except what shone from a very red nose; he was smoking a short pipe, and was painting the Virgin Mary's face. The touch was a finishing one, put on with deliberation, slowly, so that it was two or three seconds before I discovered that the interloper was no saint.
>
> (chapter XV)

The art historians, like the travellers and the tourists, have until recent years not much concerned themselves with such extravagant sculpture. But things are now changing, as was revealed by the splendid 1973 exhibition of *Il Seicento Lombardo* in Milan. At Varallo, Varese and Oropo, one is still a foreigner among Italians. But Orta, once a tranquil haven for Victorian visitors, is now again facing the modern world. A smart hotel has taken precedence of the lakeside *albergo*, with its old-fashioned comforts and exquisite view over towards the Isola di San Giulio. Brightly coloured postcards of some of the sculptures are now offered for sale—something unknown (in spite of the pilgrims) thirty or forty years ago.

The emphasis on the Italian workmanship of the supposed statue in Paulina's chapel and praise of its sculptor's art of extreme realism may be due to Shakespeare's having heard tell that, in the early seventeenth century, intensely naturalistic life-size statuary flourished in towns in Lombardy and Piedmont, where they were likely to be seen by travellers and to give them their first impressions of the wonders of contemporary Italian artistry.

Perhaps an editor's note on the passage in *The Winter's Tale* might read:

> The name 'Giulio Romano' for a skilled Italian artificer is theatrically effective. No sculptor of this name is known, but Shakespeare may have had memories of the painter and architect Giulio Romano (Giulio Pippi, 1499–1546) or the musician Giulio Romano (Giulio Caccini, *c.* 1545–1618). The latter was still alive at the time of the composition of *The Winter's Tale* and his work was known in England. Shakespeare's eye may have caught the name in Robert Dowland's recently published volume of lute-songs, *A Musicall Banquet. Furnished with varietie of delicious Ayres, Collected out of the best Authors in English, French, Spanish and Italian* (London, 1610). This was compiled from 'the rarest and most judicious Maisters' ('To the Reader'), and Nos XVIII and XIX are ascribed to *Giulio Caccini detto Romano*. The attribution of the supposed statue to an Italian, the emphasis on the extreme realism of his work, and the details used in describing it in the chapel in v. iii, may be due to Shakespeare's having heard something of recent developments in Italian sculpture. In the hill-towns of Piedmont and

Lombardy (Orta, Varallo and elsewhere), where they were likely to be seen by travellers arriving over the Alps and to provide them with first impressions of Italian artistry, life-size, painted, terra-cotta statues, of startling realism, were from the 1590s onwards being placed in a series of hill-side chapels (forming a 'Sacro Monte').

IV

Henry Vaughan's Biblical Landscape

ELUNED BROWN

The earlier poems of Henry Vaughan exhibit him most obviously as a poet of a particular landscape—that of his native Breconshire. Both *Poems* (1646) and *Olor Iscanus* (1651) have several 'local poems' in a well-established classical and Renaissance tradition of which Vaughan shows himself aware. Addressing the river Usk, he refers to the convention:

> Soft *Petrarch* (thaw'd by *Laura*'s flames) did weep
> On *Tybers* banks, when she (*proud fair!*) cou d sleep;
> *Mosella* boasts *Ausonius*, and the *Thames*
> Doth murmure SIDNEYS *Stella* to her *streams*,
> While *Severn* swoln with *Joy* and *sorrow*, wears
> *Castara*'s smiles mixt with fair *Sabrin*'s tears.[1]

Vaughan's poem to the Usk is an example of what Johnson called in his *Life of Denham* 'a species of composition that may be denominated local poetry, of which the fundamental subject is some particular landscape, to be poetically described, with the addition of such embellishments as may be supplied by historical retrospection, or incidental meditation'. Denham's poem which inspired Johnson's remark is recollected by Vaughan in his poem 'The Mount of Olives':

> *Cotswold*, and *Coopers* both have met
> With learned swaines, and Eccho yet
> Their pipes, and wit; (p. 414)

---

[1] *The Works of Henry Vaughan*, ed. L. C. Martin, 2nd edition (Oxford, 1957), p. 39.

Yet, paradoxically, Vaughan has a more obvious claim to be a local poet, a 'Silurist', in his secular than in his religious verse for which he first adopted this title. Not only the river Usk and its valley are celebrated in the volumes of secular verse, but the Priory Grove at Brecon alongside intimate portraits and recollections of Breconshire friends. The locality is described precisely, though in *formulae* that are recognizably in the 'locus amoenus' tradition, perhaps owing more to Petrarchan descriptions of his retirement at Vaucluse than is usually recognized.

Silex Scintillans (1650) was Vaughan's first publication to bear the title 'Silurist', the publication of the secular volume *Olor Iscanus* being delayed until 1651. The obvious motives for adopting such a title have been frequently rehearsed: the enforced retirement to his native county of a defeated Royalist and Anglican supporter; the preoccupation with translation of treatises dealing with retirement and country life; the distinctive nature of such a title among so many distinguished Vaughans in Wales. The Silures, as Tacitus describes them, were a tribe of Britons stubbornly resistant to an alien Roman yoke and it may well be that Vaughan's title alludes not only to his local 'pietas' but to the heroic past of the Silures which he felt to be particularly pertinent at the time of his own defeat and mental and spiritual resistance. Certainly all subsequent volumes punctiliously observe his self-styled title, as do his friends in printed commendation.

Attitudes to landscape in the religious poetry are coloured by 'historical retrospection', to use Johnson's phrase, in a very special sense. Nature in general and the local landscape in particular is transformed into a recognizable biblical and indeed Middle-Eastern landscape. What may be described as 'baptized Breconshire' has drawn observation but not the extended critical comment that other aspects of Vaughan's treatment of the natural world have excited. It is not my intention to diminish or challenge those studies that place a great deal of emphasis on the Hermetic strain in Vaughan's vocabulary and thinking, nor to ignore the way in which the landscape is allegorically treated for meditative purposes. There is abundant evidence in Vaughan's own work for the importance of these approaches without the necessity of invoking the work of his twin, Thomas Vaughan. The influence of his writings needs, however, to be set alongside some of Vaughan's explicit statements about the primacy of Scripture (and by implication his Church) and the cautionary warnings of a friend, Thomas Powell, as demonstrably close to him in religious matters as his brother:

> while we wander in vain fantasies, following after new notions, or new-nothings, Chymical and Chymical Divinity and such quelques-choses to please the fastidious and irregular appetites of this age, we are bewildered, like Travellers that disdaining the beaten and obvious road-waies are always seeking short-cuts . . .
>
> (*Quadriga Salutis*, 1657)

I should like to reassert the primacy of the 'beaten and obvious road-waies' to Vaughan. Much Hermetic vocabulary is biblical in origin, though, of course, gaining a special intensity through its significance in loosely-Hermetic writing. 'Father of lights' in the poem, normally interpreted in Hermetic terms, is a direct biblical quotation which is meditated upon in association with the historical significance of 'Cock-Crowing'. M. M. Mahood in her *Poetry and Humanism* (1950) conjectures that even in the seventeenth century 'there is no poet of the period whose work reveals a more intimate knowledge of the Bible' (p. 255). Vaughan's biblical allusions are certainly more recondite than those of Donne or Herbert or Crashaw and he is less typological in his linking of Old and New Testaments. Vaughan's biblical emphasis is more overt in the second volume of *Silex Scintillans* with a number of poems commenting explicitly on a biblical text and biblical events being pressed as models for the acute problems of moral behaviour experienced by Vaughan in the Commonwealth period. Significantly the penultimate poem of the volume is addressed to the Holy Bible:

Thou overcam'st my sinful strength,
And having brought me home, didst there
Shew me that pearl I sought elsewhere.[1]

The unimaginatively dependent use of Scripture in volume II is, nevertheless, a weakness and many of the Scriptural poems have been neglected in favour of those that yield more glamorous interpretation. Vaughan's poem to Holy Scripture in volume I is, however, moving in its combination of wit and feeling:

O that I had deep Cut in my hard heart
    Each line in thee! Then would I plead in groans
    Of my Lords penning, and by sweetest Art
Return upon himself the *Law*, and *Stones*.[2]

This quotation nicely demonstrates the relationship between the Incarnate word, the Word of God in Scripture, and the poet as the creation of God who is himself reflecting the creative act in his life and work.

The Bible (as traditionally interpreted) is not only the starting point for many of Vaughan's lesser poems, but also shapes in a profound way many of the major ones. There is ample precedent among Christian poets for the use of the Bible as a literary model. Not only Milton, but also Donne drew attention to the literary skill in Scripture. He, in common with St Augustine and Petrarch, was particularly devoted to the Psalms:

a man may have a particular love towards such or such a book of Scripture, and in such affection, I acknowledge that my spirituall appetite carries me still, upon the *Psalms of David* . . . which is such a form as is both curious, and requires diligence in the making, and then when it is made, can have nothing, no syllable taken from it, nor added to it:[3]

[1] Vaughan, op. cit., p. 541.
[2] Vaughan, op. cit., p. 441.
[3] G. Potter and E. Simpson (eds.), *Sermons of John Donne* (University of California Press, Berkeley and Los Angeles, 1955), II, pp. 49–50.

The Psalmes are the Manna of the Church. As Manna tasted to every man like that that he liked best, so doe the Psalmes minister Instruction, and satisfaction, to every man, in every emergency and occasion. *David* was not onely a cleare Prophet of Christ himselfe, but a Prophet of every particular Christian;[1]

The importance of the Psalter in Anglican devotion does not need stressing nor its importance as the archetypal devotional poetry so often translated and paraphrased in this period. Vaughan's own translations though not distinguished in language are significant in choice: 65, 104 and 121. These are the Psalms which most explore the relation between the Psalmist and God-in-Nature, in terms both of praise and rejoicing and sober meditation. Furthermore, many phrases of the Psalter lie behind Vaughan's most celebrated Poems though they are rarely called on to explicate them. 'The Morning Watch' not only echoes Vaughan's devotional work *The Mount of Olives* but also Psalm 130: 'My soul fleeth unto the Lord: before the morning watch, I say before the morning watch'. As well as St John and the mystic writers the Psalmist comments on the mysterious darkness of God in Psalm 18: 'He made darkness his secret place; his pavilion round him with dark water, and thick cloud to cover him' and in Psalm 139: 'Yea, the darkness is no darkness with thee, but the night is as clear as the day'.[2] Both these texts illuminate Vaughan's poem 'The Night' and even the celebrated image in 'The Retreate' may owe something to Psalm 107 where the sailors reel to and fro and 'stagger like a drunken man'. Verbal allusions are plentiful and direct quotation from the Psalms possibly predominates in Vaughan over other biblical echoes.

Much more important than these possibly accidental allusions, or even direct quotation, is the influence of the Psalter on the subject matter of Vaughan's poetry, particularly in the directions in which he differs from Herbert. The preoccupation of many

[1] Ibid., VII, p. 51.
[2] Quotations from the Psalms are from *The Book of Common Prayer*.

Psalms with God-in-Nature or the spiritual landscape of the soul is expressed in many images that frequently occur in Vaughan: 'the hills from whence cometh help'; 'all my springs are in thee'; 'My soul thirsteth for thee, my flesh also longeth after thee, in a barren and dry land where no water is'; 'The righteous shall flourish like a palm tree'; 'who turned the hard rock into standing water and the flint stone into a springing well'.

The many references to clouds, water from rock, pillars of fire must be related not only to the story of the pilgrimage of the children of Israel to the Promised Land but also to the second preoccupation which the Psalmist shares with Vaughan—God-in-history—particularly during the time of the Patriarchs. Vaughan's interest in this period of the 'white' days of the Patriarch is much deeper than a pious celebration of those heroes of faith such as the writer to the Hebrews describes and who are subsequently invoked in countless commentaries and sermons. The expulsion from Eden, the bondage in Egypt and the journey to the Promised Land received specifically Christian interpretation in terms of sin and redemption (particularly in baptismal and Easter rites) in liturgy and commentary. Yet Vaughan's interest is not wholly explained by reference to this tradition. In the period in which he wrote the sense of desolation, even of the way in which God seemed to hide his face, is acute. The 'easy' revelation of God seemed to Vaughan not simply a blessing of Eden but of the Patriarchs:

> In *Abr'hams* Tent the winged guests
> (O how familiar then was heaven!)
> Eate, drinke, discourse, sit downe, and rest
> Untill the Coole, and shady *Even*;[1]
>
> Sure, it was so. Man in those early days
>   Was not all stone, and Earth . . .
> Nor was Heav'n cold unto him; for each day
>   The vally, or the Mountain
> Afforded visits, and still *Paradise* lay
>   In some green shade, or fountain.

[1] Vaughan, op. cit., p. 404.

> Angels lay *Leiger* here; Each Bush, and Cel,
>   Each Oke, and high-way knew them,
> Walk but the fields, or sit down at some *wel*,
>   And he was sure to view them.[1]

The loss of this familiarity is a general loss of mankind who long to know and see God face to face. Vaughan's images of mists and shadows, masques and shades gather some force from Platonic and Neoplatonic associations but are more fundamentally related to the ways in which God revealed himself—or hid himself as described in the Old Testament—in narrative and in meditative comment as in the Psalms. The richest images are those of the 'veil', our flesh which removes us from direct knowledge for the time being.

> But that great darkness at thy death
> When the Veyl broke with thy last breath,
> Did make us to see
> The way to thee;[2]

> Onely this Veyle which thou hast broke,
> And must be broken yet in me
> This veyle I say, is all the cloke
> And cloud which shadows thee from me.[3]

The Patriarchs' knowledge of God is enviable and glimpsed only momentarily in childhood, in sacraments and the symphony of nature. Yet even these are but 'lights weak minority'.

The 'white days' of the Old Testament heroes are intensely recovered by Vaughan and one feels for more than convenient types of innocent knowledge of God. Many of the references carry overtones of Vaughan's particular sense of religious deprivation in the Commonwealth period, as well as the expected sense of loss experienced by fallen mankind:

[1] Vaughan, op. cit., p. 440.
[2] Vaughan, op. cit., p. 458.
[3] Vaughan, op. cit., p. 489.

We have no Conf'rence in these daies: . . .

So poison'd, breaks forth in some Clime,
And at first sight doth many please,
But drunk, is puddle, or meere slime
And 'stead of Phisick, a disease;

Just such a tainted sink we have
Like that Samaritans dead Well . . .[1]

The many allusions to Jacob's stony pillow coalesce in 'Jacob's
pillow and pillar' and Vaughan's comparison of the plight of
Jacob with his own:

But blessed Jacob, though thy sad distress
Was just the same with ours, and nothing less;
For thou a brother, and blood-thirsty too
Didst flye, whose children wrought thy childrens wo:
Yet thou in all thy solitude and grief,
On stones didst sleep and found'st but cold relief;[2]

The struggles of the early Patriarchs are nearer Vaughan's own
condition than their enviable discourse with God and he identifies
with the struggles of Jacob and Ishmael 'the weeping lad'. Their
hallowed places (before the building of the Temple) are as much
part of his landscape as his own neighbourhood. So Bethel, the
well of Sychar, the miraculous well that quenched the thirst of
Hagar and Ishmael, Eschol's brook, the plains of Mamre, the holy
mountains are juxtaposed with the 'drowsie lake' (possibly Llan-
gors lake), the cromlech of Ty Illtyd (in 'Vanity of Spirit') or
Pen-y-Fan, the highest point of the Beacons which is wittily
referred to in 'The Dawning'.[3] This easy assimilation of the history
of Israel (also of course suggesting the life of all Christians) to
the present concerns of the poet finds an obvious parallel in the
Psalter. Although Vaughan reads as a Christian, interpreting the
Old Testament in the light of the New, there is close attention to

[1] Vaughan, op. cit., p. 404.
[2] Vaughan, op. cit., p. 528.
[3] This suggestion by W. M. Merchant was recorded by Martin in the 2nd
edition, pp. 739–40.

the literal sense and an independent appreciation of Judaism which finds sad expression in 'The Jews'.

Vaughan's religious poetry, then, shares at least two concerns with the Psalmist: the relation between the individual soul and God's creation and between the individual and God's dealings with his chosen people. To some extent both these themes are concerned with the recovery of lost innocence and glory but Vaughan's main emphasis comes to be on the revealed fulfilment of redemption at the Last Day.

The longing for the righteous judgment of God and joy at its manifestation is the theme of several Psalms: 'Let the field be joyful and all the trees of the wood shall rejoice before the Lord for he cometh, for he cometh to judge the earth'. Vaughan, too, expresses more joy than traditional dread at the idea of judgment. But to pursue the parallel in attitude too far is to do no more than argue that 'there are salmons in both'. The Psalmist rejoices at the defeat of enemies and the return of equity. Moreover, on the literal level at least, there is considerable confidence at the defeat of unspecified enemies and relish in their discomfiture. Allowing for the Christian reading of this as the final defeat of Satan, Vaughan's tone is very different. His view of the political and religious situation of the 1650s seems at times to visualize only an eschatalogical resolution. The triumphs of AntiChrist cause most anguish as an aspect of the continuing passion of Christ. But his anti-militarism is apparent in 'Men of War':

> The sword wherewith thou dost command
> Is in thy mouth, not in thy hand . . .
>
> Give me, my God! a heart as milde,
> And plain, as when I was a childe;
> That when *thy Throne* is set, and all
> These *Conquerors* before it fall
> I may be found (preserv'd by thee)
> Who by no blood (here) overcame
> But the blood of the *blessed Lamb*.[1]

[1] Vaughan, op. cit., pp. 517–18.

The Judgment Day that is longed for will not simply bring justice but will be the fulfilment of all Creation including man:

> And through thy creatures pierce and pass
> Till all becomes thy cloudless glass,
> Transparent as the purest day
> And without blemish or decay,
> Fixt by thy spirit to a state
> For evermore immaculate.
> A state fit for the sight of thy
> Immediate, pure and unveil'd eye,
> A state agreeing with thy minde,
> A state thy birth, and death design'd:
> A state for which thy creatures all
> Travel and groan, and look and call.[1]

The confidence in the defeat of the enemy is there and often the enemy can refer only to the Puritan rulers but the tone carries more bewildered pain than anticipated triumph. The specific references to the Puritans are more numerous in volume II though it would be wrong to associate all the judgment poems with Vaughan's personal attitudes. The landscape of judgment owes a great deal to the Psalms (and of course to Revelations) but it also has a particular location in the poet's own surroundings. The use of the demonstrative adjective in conjunction with natural features is prominent in Vaughan: 'that drowsie lake', 'this hill', 'that stream', 'this bank', and this habit extends into the poems concerned with the Last Things:

> Or those faint beams in which this hill is drest,
> After the Sun's remove.

> Either disperse these mists, which blot and fill
> My perspective (still) as they pass,
> Or else remove me hence unto that hill,
> Where I shall need no glass.[2]

[1] Vaughan, op. cit., p. 542.
[2] Vaughan, op. cit., p. 484.

The landscape, however allegorically read, profoundly studied or historically viewed, receives its final transformation at Judgment Day when its essentially 'metaphoric' character is realized and in Vaughan's eyes the shadows obtain substance.

V

Blake's Mixed Media: a Mixed Blessing

G. INGLI JAMES

WHAT Hagstrum and others refer to as Blake's composite art has long been a source of interest and admiration. As early as Cunningham's *Life* there is mention of the way poetry and painting are 'interwoven' in the illuminated writings. Smethman, in the 1860s, talks about pages whose effect is to leave the mind 'in pleasant uncertainty as to whether it is a picture that is singing, or a song which has newly blossomed into colour and form'. W. M. Rossetti, in his edition of 1874, remarks on 'an intermixture of art and poetry so intimate that the union of the two becomes something different from ... mere mechanical juxtaposition'. If there is anything new in the current preoccupation with the subject it is only that the scholarly and critical discussion is so much more detailed and informed than it used to be. Earlier explorers tend not to have travelled very much in the realms of gold, merely to have glimpsed them. George Leonard, sometime professor at the University of Bristol, is fairly representative. Speaking at the first meeting of the Blake Society, at Hampstead, in 1912, he urged the members, among whom was the young Geoffrey Keynes, '*somehow* ... to see the *Songs of Innocence and Experience*, as Blake meant you to see them ... songs and pictures together'. In one, he went on, 'belonging to the Linnell collection, *which I saw on Saturday*, all the sheep are touched over with gold ... *If I remember rightly*, the soft brown ink of the lettering is written over with gold'.[1] If, after this, one turns to Erdman and Grant's *Blake's Visionary Forms Dramatic*, one is bound to be impressed by the number of trained observers now returning from the world of the illuminated books, complete with notes, maps and detailed

[1] *The First Meeting of The Blake Society, Papers* (my italics), (Olney, 1912), pp. 46–7.

photographic evidence. The scene is becoming very familiar. At the same time, however, the vast majority of Blake enthusiasts still haven't been there themselves; and even the specialist occasionally has problems. Erdman tells us that he was able to reach firm conclusions about certain plates from *The Marriage of Heaven and Hell* because of 'the fortunate opportunity to examine six of the nine copies . . . in pairs side by side within the same few weeks'.[1] This is a far cry from George Leonard, it is true; but obviously difficulties of access continue to exist at all levels. Albion may be awake, but entry into Jerusalem is still more or less restricted. And now that we are all more inclined to find fault with ourselves than with the artist, one may be forgiven perhaps for insisting that in this case it is the nature of the terrain that is to blame. Ironically, it is Blake's mixing of the media that is responsible both for the attraction and the restriction.

There is of course no reason why the arts of poetry and painting should not be successfully united between the covers of an illustrated book. But the artist must recognize that a book, if it is to be capable of reaching an audience of reasonable size, cannot afford to be rare in the way an oil-painting or water-colour normally is. A painting may be unique; but because the owner may safely and conveniently share it with many others—merely by exhibiting it —its rarity doesn't in itself make it unavailable. Merely to exhibit a book, on the other hand, is not enough: if the owner is to share it he must allow it to be handled and borrowed; and because of the risk and inconvenience involved this is not likely to happen on a significant scale. A book, therefore, if it is not to be limited to a single owner and his immediate circle, needs to be published—as indeed most of them are, even the most lavish and exotic—in the form of an edition of more or less numerous copies, so that there may be multiple owners. And hence the unsuitability of painting in its 'pure' form to the illustration of an extended text. The two elements combined merely frustrate each other, painting being a medium which inhibits reproduction and demands display, whilst a text is something which inhibits

---

[1] David V. Erdman (ed.), *The Illuminated Blake* (O.U.P. 1975), p. 15.

display and demands reproduction. In Eden their loves may have been the same, here they are opposite, and the only practical solution is for one or the other to accept a subordinate role and adapt to the needs of its partner. Susan Langer's view that there are no marriages of the arts, only successful rapes, is to this extent sound. Thus a text might be successfully incorporated into a painting, but only if it were brief enough to appear, in reasonably large letters, on one side of a canvas. (A rough analogy would be the modern poster-poem.) Alternatively, pictorial designs may be satisfactorily integrated into a book, but only if the artist accommodates himself to the book's need for copies, by relying heavily on one or more of the printmaking processes, such as etching or engraving. The result of an artist failing to do so may be seen in the extreme inaccessibility of Blake's water-colour illustrations to the poems of Gray.

We talk about 'the unique copy' of *Blake's Gray*, formerly belonging to the Duke of Hamilton. But strictly speaking, until the facsimiles of 1922 and 1972 there was no such thing as a *copy* of these designs: like most works in the same medium they were simply unique. Nor would this have been a serious limitation had they really been suitable for public display. But being illustrations to a text of over a hundred pages, to which they were physically joined, they were part of something which asked to be held and perused at close quarters. The format, that is to say, demands ownership, not exhibition; but ownership is severely limited by the inherent difficulty of reproduction. The desire to produce a facsimile *edition* was as natural as the high price was inevitable. Equally understandable was the decision of the Trianon Press to offer their edition in two forms: 'either bound in three half-morocco volumes ... or separate as plates suitable for display'. The *Gray* is a hybrid, whose two components pull in opposite directions. And the fact that it is not naturally suited either to exhibition or to reproduction means that it can be made available only to an extremely limited number of people.

In fairness to Blake it must be admitted that the *Gray* was a special order, and that with Flaxman as the only customer it made more sense to employ water-colour as a medium than to etch or engrave a plate from which multiple impressions could be taken. This is a case, therefore, where neglect of an artist in his own day helped to produce something incapable of becoming widely known, in its true and original form, even after he had come into fashion. (By contrast, a neglected painting has usually only to be discovered.) Almost as important, however, may have been Blake's own inclinations. For a person whose gifts and aspirations in the realm of fine art were as pronounced as his, there must always have been a temptation to allow the painter in him more scope than is appropriate to an illuminated book. Thus quite apart from the chosen medium, there is the sheer size of the 116 *Gray* sheets (the 1922 facsimile is an unwieldy elephant folio), suggesting that the artist simply turned a blind eye to the fact that they would need to be handled like the pages of any other book. As a result, the work was inaccessible not only to the general public but also, to some extent, one imagines, to the fortunate owner himself. Astonishment has been expressed that it was completely lost to sight for a hundred years; but its physical make-up alone was almost sufficient to ensure that it would soon be put to one side, and eventually forgotten. And now that Irene Tayler and others have alerted us to how exciting the relationship between text and design can be, it is important not to forget that whatever the aesthetic and intellectual appeal of the work, Blake's way of mixing the media has distinct drawbacks from a practical point of view.

The same is true of the books in which Blake illuminated his own text—even though here he had hoped initially for a sizeable audience, and had therefore had the need for copies, and hence for printmaking, very much in mind. Indeed, the whole project hinged, as is well known, on his discovery of how he could use relief etching to print letterpress as well as designs. His belief, in 1793, that he had found an inexpensive means of providing 'the public' with beautiful books was of course naïvely optimistic, especially in view of some of the laborious techniques involved, such as step-biting. But makers of rare books are notorious for cherishing illusions (*vide* the professed aim of the Gregynog Press to 'cultivate a love of beautiful things in the people of Wales . . .

and not increase the specimens accumulated by collectors'). What makes Blake's case especially ironical is that in spite of his hopes and intentions he turned out volumes which, by their very nature, couldn't match even the very limited circulation of press books of the usual type. Instead of *copies*, more or less numerous, he produced a handful of more or less differing *versions* of any given work. The plate was liable to alteration at any time, and what was done in the way of colouring varied enormously. Erdman, speaking of 'how distinctive each copy is in colouring and in the finishing details', suggests that some of them were tailored to individual buyers: 'a picture made explicit and shared with one or two customers, close friends who will not laugh or will laugh in the right way'. In effect, Blake was 'issuing different editions for different customers'[1]—using 'edition' in a figurative sense. That is to say, although the illuminated books did utilize a printmaking process, in the end it was overlaid and absorbed by procedures which nullified its reproductive capacity.

They are not of course the only works in which Blake, whilst employing a method of printing, is nevertheless more painter than printer. In creating his so-called colour-printed drawings, or monotypes, he transferred an image from millboard to paper in a way which allowed only about three impressions to be taken, each one fainter than its predecessors, and therefore requiring more finishing in pen and water-colour. Clearly he was interested in the technique, as Butlin says, 'more for its textural qualities than as a means of reproduction';[2] and Tatham indeed was of the opinion that it was just because the impression varied slightly, encouraging him to 'branch out so as to make each one different' that Blake found it so attractive. In short, like many creative artists when they turn to printmaking, he was more interested in the effects he could obtain than in merely repeating the effect. But the monotypes are not books: they are pictures, made to be displayed. The fact that to all intents and purposes there are no copies doesn't limit unreasonably the size of their audience. On the walls of the Tate

[1] Ibid., pp. 15-16.
[2] Martin Butlin, *William Blake: A Complete Catalogue of the Works in the Tate Gallery* (The Tate Gallery, 1971), p. 34.

Gallery they may safely and conveniently be made available to numberless viewers. With books it is different. By so subduing the printmaking and reproductive element that, as W. H. Stevenson says, he 'never made the same book twice', Blake may well have demonstrated his loathing of Urizenic monotony, as Erdman suggests. But the crippling price a book has to pay for uniqueness is to become as inaccessible as a painting that cannot be exhibited.

Again it was lack of demand that largely determined what happened. Although he had set out with Albion in mind, customers for the illuminated books were few and far between. And since he usually left at least the hand-colouring until a purchaser appeared, this meant that he was able to give individual 'copies' the kind of attention that would have been impossible if orders had been pouring in. In fact, the more obvious it became that reproduction was not going to be an important factor, the more elaborate his colour-schemes tended to grow. Gilchrist tells of kind friends who, choosing to pay the artist more than he asked, were favoured with plates finished like miniatures. Lister estimates that when it came to *Jerusalem*, for which there was no buyer in view, he must have worked on it for several hours a week over a period of nine years, since each of the coloured plates represents 'as much effort as that required to produce an elaborately-wrought water-colour of the same size'.[1] Blake's comment to Cumberland ('to Print it will Cost my Time the amount of Twenty Guineas. One I have finish'd. It contains 100 Plates but it is not likely that I shall get a Customer for it') contrasts painfully with his earlier hopes for the illuminated books, and helps to show how, as the possibility of an audience evaporated, he tended to push them increasingly in the direction of paintings. It was a natural enough thing for a painter-poet to do, and especially in Blake's case. The aspiring painter who had had to settle at an early age for print-making as a living, and whose ideals were in any case so different from those of the Academy, must instinctively have welcomed any opportunity—even the one provided by shortage of customers—to demonstrate his very finest art. Unfortunately, within the

[1] Raymond Lister, *Infernal Methods: A Study of William Blake's Art Techniques* (Bell, 1975), p. 80.

context of a book the result was bound to be mixed: something at once extraordinarily beautiful and excessively rare.

And again, as with the *Gray*, difficulties of access, in a sense, awaited even the reader who could get hold of the work. Size is not a problem in the illuminated books, but legibility sometimes is, and not only because the letterpress is not in conventional type. Gilchrist's comment on the *Songs of Innocence and Experience* deserves to stand:

> A few were issued plain, in black and white, or blue and white, which are more legible than the polychrome examples. In these latter, the red or yellow lettering being sometimes unrelieved by a white ground, we have, instead of contrasted hue, gradations of it, as in a picture.[1]

When, in addition, the text and designs physically intermingle in the manner we so admire, the difficulty can be exacerbated. The visual effect is often strikingly beautiful. But it would be disingenuous to pretend that our attempt properly to attend to the marks on the page is never seriously impeded. The reason, after all, why the most popular facsimiles have included with the reproductions an ordinary printing of the text, isolated from the designs, is that most readers need it. What has happened, in fact, is that the art of the illustrator has so embraced the text that it tends at times to suffocate it. One can understand how it came about. Apart from any illusions he had about being able to produce fine books inexpensively, the use of relief-etching for words as well as pictures must have seemed particularly appropriate in view of the fact that both were his own. One suspects too that his own words in his own hand seemed legible to him even in places where they had been too completely drawn into a coloured and crowded picture. But if a book is to be read by others there are limits beyond which the picture-maker must take care not to go. Because he was inclined to subordinate the printer to the painter, and the poet's text to both, Blake went so far as to create volumes which are not only difficult to reproduce but also, at times, to read.

[1] Gilchrist's *Life of Blake*, ed. Todd (Dent, 1942), p. 105.

Nor, finally, should it be imagined that modern facsimiles have virtually solved the problems of access. It is not simply that the best reproductions are inevitably such fine and expensive works that they are themselves difficult to come by. (Keynes is being somewhat unrealistic when he talks of 'the ordinary man' looking to libraries to make them available'.[1] Few institutions can afford, and none is likely to permit large numbers of people actually to handle, books of which the *Times Literary Supplement* has said: 'they will in the future be the treasures of libraries'.) More important is the fact that no facsimile is ever a perfect substitute for the original, and that Blake, above all, has urged the importance of being faithful down to the minutest particular. More important still, perhaps, is that even if absolute accuracy were possible, we still couldn't expect, even from the Blake Trust, facsimiles of each of the so-called copies of any given work: yet this is really what we need. As John E. Grant says: 'the variation in rendering of details is such that no serious scholar should try to make pronouncements about iconography until he has carefully compared a considerable number of copies'.[2] Erdman's *Illuminated Blake* is, it is true, packed with verbal information about variants: one can learn from him, if one did not already know, that the sick rose, for example, in Copy Y of the *Songs*, is not crimson but white; that the large bunch of grapes in *Earth's Answer* is not present in Copy Z, and so on. But valuable as Erdman's edition is, it is still a long way from the real thing. Like any attempt to make the illuminated works more widely known, it has had to be content with making them much less than fully known. Edward J. Rose was no doubt right when he said that

> it will serve those best who do not really need it, since it will be used most often as a memory stimulator by those who already know the originals (as well as the Trianon facsimiles) or have access to a representative number of them.[3]

[1] See Sir Geoffrey Keynes's Supplementary Note in *William Blake: Poems and Prophecies*, ed. Max Plowman (Dent, 1959), p. xxviii.
[2] *Blake Newsletter* 6 (15 Sept., 1968), p. 30.
[3] *Blake Newsletter* 34 (Fall, 1975), p. 54.

The comment is a devastating reflection, not on Erdman but on the extent to which Blake's composite art frustrates its own need for reproduction. The *Job*, his supreme achievement in many ways, is different in this respect, as are the *Night Thoughts* engravings; but what we normally mean by the illuminated books are all characterized by this inherent contradiction, which keeps them shut up from the world. In their case, Max Plowman's remark that Blake will inevitably 'come into his own *when the world is ready for him*' doesn't apply. Because of the complex circumstances which shaped them—largely indeed because of Blake's multiple gifts as poet, printer, painter and prophet—they have long been a heaven on earth for the wealthy bibliophile and the bibliographer (Urizen has had a field-day). To others, with very few exceptions, they must remain a promised land, seen with the aid of a photographer's glass, more or less darkly. Earth is no longer turning away, but the starry floor, the wat'ry shore is still what is given us, till the break of day.

VI

The Painter and Literature

JOSEF HERMAN

I LEARNT to read at the age of four. A man of great charity, Dr Zaltzman, of whom I have written at some length in my book *Related Twilights*, taught me how to put letters together; since then there has hardly been a day during which I have not read something. However, my mind was affected by books, sometimes even poisoned, when I would have to turn to other books to wash away much of the poison; yet, however my mind may have been instructed—I love ideas—my heart remained illiterate and essentially primitive.

Delacroix writes somewhere in his *Journals*: 'To set aflame your imagination, read always Shakespeare and Byron'. It worked with the Romantics. I tried it; perhaps I was too young, but it did not work with me. Reading absorbs me completely, my imagination and all; but it does not urge me to work. The urgent flame which makes me paint must come from life itself. I paint emotions which I do not find in reading. In this too I am a primitive. Painting has come down to us from pre-lingual times. Still today it is akin to dancing or miming, a 'silent language' with its own basic signs.

Yet I remember one occasion when I painted a picture that was closely coordinated with a book. This was a rare adventure worth telling. Some years back my friend Moelwyn Merchant stayed with me for a weekend. My small family and I then lived in Suffolk. We had long talks, Merchant and I. At one point he said that the Arts Council had asked him to mount an exhibition, 'Shakespeare and the Arts', for the four hundredth anniversary of Shakespeare's birth and he asked me to paint a picture in time for this exhibition.

'What about something from *Lear*?' he asked, hinting, perhaps suggesting, perhaps trying to stimulate my emotions.

'Maybe, yes, this appeals to me ... something from *Lear*,' I mumbled. The weekend ended and Merchant left.

I read and re-read *Lear* about a dozen times. The more I read it the more I was convinced that following the text would lead me nowhere, to an illustration perhaps, but nothing more significant. I put the book aside and began brooding over something more like a synthesis. In this mood I was sitting at a table facing a blank page. Half dreaming I felt my hand making circular movements ... I soon had the shape of a bundle. A sad, human bundle. Now I got excited, my imagination 'inflamed' in the way Delacroix so thoughtfully described the process. Now I saw clearly everything I had to draw. Eventually the human bundle lay passively midst rocks and stones on bare earth, a heath on which nothing could grow. With this much to go by, I began painting. In the distance, far from the human bundle, on the horizon, I painted the Fool sitting on a low heap of pebbles, playing a flute, totally unconcerned with Lear's fate. The sky, lyrical and soft, an eventide all rose and red, the colour of a peach; like the Fool, nature too was unconcerned with Lear's lot. Lear was intensely alone ...

There exists no such scene in Shakespeare's *King Lear*. But everything in the second act suggests the gradual intensification of Lear's loneliness and grief which culminates in the wretchedness of madness. Except for the moment of dying, human isolation cannot go further.

Here we come to the crux of the matter of the relationship between literature and art. Literature can awaken the creative energies of the painter—but so can a few raindrops on a windowpane. This is clearly not the object of literature and is quite accidental in its nature.

Each medium has a life of its own; as with the word, so with paint. The singularity of the medium decides its processes and makes of each art something special, something different, something unique. For both the writer and the painter the level of experience may be the same. Even their inner resources and the quality of the imagination may be the same; yet the relationship to the experience will undergo a transformation because of the necessity of the writer to use words, or of the painter to make of his experience a tangible image true to the materiality of paint. The painter's communion with the material is decisive for the meaning and the spirituality of his image. Whatever the central emphasis, the process of writing allows a variety of descriptive viewpoints, even contradictory beliefs and moods. In painting, no matter how varied its implications, the image is a compressed entity confined to one single mood on one single surface. But more significant than this: in the process of articulating his quest, the individual *voice* of the writer is of supreme importance; no individual voice—no style, no story, no book. Now this individual voice, so different from writer to writer, is the greatest miracle in the art of writing. It is not the same as the writer's day-to-day speaking voice. It is probably the voice suggested by the controlled rhythm of phrasing—or perhaps something still more complicated. What in literature is the writer's voice is in painting the individual way of handling paint, which results in a specific surface texture and an individual line in the form. No specific texture—no individual line, no style, no picture; even the most abstract idea comes to life through the textural and formal concreteness. From it the viewer will derive all the purity of spontaneous sensations. That it can do this is the miracle of painting.

And in spite of all the irreconcilable differences between art and literature—these of which I have spoken are but the very basic ones—their object is the same: to sharpen our sense of wonder, to sharpen our sense of life.

VII

Edgar Allan Poe and the Early Avant-Garde Film

MIKE WEAVER

IN 1928 and 1929 two silent film versions of Poe's *The Fall of the House of Usher* were in production; the first was being made in Paris by Jean Epstein and the second in the United States by James Sibley Watson, Jr. Both films were important contributions to the avant-garde film in its first phase, but they may also be considered as creative criticisms of Poe's original story, illuminating not only its themes but also the presentation of those themes, as the transfer takes place from one medium to the other. Epstein and Watson represented two different but interwoven strands of the contemporary avant-garde. To characterize their basic styles in terms of the existing tendencies of the time one can say that Epstein's film is a Symbolist and Expressionist work, while Watson's is Cubo-Futurist. Epstein was a film dramatist in the main stream of the French avant-garde while Watson followed the minor purist tributary of Léger and Man Ray. They were united in their rejection of the influence of *The Cabinet of Dr Caligari* (1919), although when they came to suggest what kind of a painter Roderick Usher was they both fell back on a style which was unmistakably German Expressionist.

Jean Epstein, who was born in Warsaw in 1897 of French and Polish parentage, formed his own film company in 1926 after some experience as an assistant director. That year he gave Luis Buñuel his first job in film as an assistant on a film of George Sand's *Mauprat*. In February 1927 he took him on again to work on *La Chute de la Maison Usher*. Epstein's interest in Poe was profound and his film was intended to relieve his long-standing obsession with Poe's whole work, and not just the single story of his title.[1]

[1] Jean Epstein, *Ecrits sur le cinéma*, 2 vols. (Paris, 1974), 1: 238 (other volume and page references are in the text).

He was not, of course, the first Frenchman to be preoccupied with Poe. From Baudelaire to Mallarmé and Valéry the line extends into the twentieth century with Debussy, who was working on an opera of *The Fall of the House of Usher* for more than ten years before his death in 1918. Debussy's interest seems to date from about 1890, as does Maeterlinck's.[1] At the same time, probably between 1893 and 1897, Edvard Munch was making paintings, etchings and lithographs of 'The Kiss', 'Vampire' and 'Attraction', which, despite his avowal that Poe and Dostoievski were the greatest influences in his life, have never been recognized for what they are—variations on the theme of the 'love' between the Ushers.

In Epstein's opinion Baudelaire's translations of Poe were dry, unfeeling and not faithful to the 'music'. Furthermore, he had contributed, through his own personality, to the view of Poe as artist of the macabre and horrible when in fact the sense of horror in Poe came as much from the living as the dead; a fragile, grey half-world between life and death was central to Poe's work (1:188). Camille Mauclair's book *La Génie d'Edgar Poe* (1925) also attacked Baudelaire as well as psychoanalytic accounts of Poe's literary powers. It tried to see the work whole, from a Symbolist point of view, emphasizing a method of composition which asserted an aesthetic sanity no matter how wretched the artist's life.[2] Poe's method is gradually to take the reader from a common-sense perception of reality to an extraordinary vision of the world without his properly knowing how it has happened. The imponderable and imperceptible mean everything. Epstein claimed this as the method of his film: 'At no time in the film will the viewer be able to say: That's slow motion' (1:191). In fact, he is wrong—there *are* moments—but on the whole the changes of speed are indeed barely perceptible. Epstein valued this technique as a means of presenting the fragile and mystical.

In a lecture of 1924, 'For a new avant-garde', Epstein denounced various abuses in the contemporary cinema, of which the excessive

---

[1] Edward Lockspeiser, *Debussy et Edgar Poe* (Monaco, 1961), pp. 49–50.
[2] See Patrick F. Quinn, *The French Face of Edgar Allan Poe* (Carbondale, 1957), pp. 56–61.

use of décor, or a reliance on theatrical sets, was the most important. He attacked *Caligari* as a still-life in which all the living elements had been killed off by brush-strokes (1:149). Its painted shadows were a sin against the moving light which was the essence of cinema because it made film mechanical and physical instead of 'photogenic'—instead of 'photographer of the illusions of the heart'. In a passage suggesting the Symbolist attitude towards objects he spoke of valuing everyday objects not for themselves but for the memories and feelings they evoked (1:150). Compare the view of the visitor-narrator of Poe's story who concludes 'that while, beyond doubt, there *are* combinations of very simple objects which have the power of thus affecting us, still the analysis of this power lies among considerations beyond our depth'. The technical process which Epstein used to develop these ideas about the object as symbol was slow motion; to capture the soul in slow motion was his aim. He was even willing to neglect purist graphic effects in favour of what he called the dramaturgy of time, the ultra-drama of slow motion (1:191). Systematically, but unobtrusively employed, it not only allowed the viewer to scan the expressions of the characters as if with a magnifying glass but also dramatized those expressions automatically. The face in close-up was like an ever-changing landscape, 'the eye-lid, with lashes you can count, is décor altered every second by emotion. From beneath the eyelid shoots the glance which is the very character of the play, and more than character—a personality' (1:149).

Epstein's film opens with the visitor on his way to the House of Usher through a murky landscape pitted with stagnant pools. He arrives at a wayside inn where he appears to the locals as an intruder as he reads with the aid of a magnifying glass a letter in which we discern with him the words 'inquiet' and 'Madeline'. Sudden appearances of a woman with a coffee pot, horrified that he is on his way to the Ushers, of another wandering in a corridor as if sleep-walking, two more with faces pressed to the window-pane so that their faces create a distorted, almost psychotic image, together with a drinker lounging contemptuously in a corner, prologue the spiritual malaise of the Ushers.

The first shot we have of Roderick is in the context of a portrait that he is painting of Madeline. Epstein has incorporated Poe's story 'The Oval Portrait', which is about a man who keeps his wife locked up in a castle while he paints her, so successfully transferring her life to the canvas that he paints her, literally, to death. Our first view of Roderick is of his hands, tightly clasped together, then of his face with a determined, obsessive expression. Madeline appears to us with a fleur-de-lis on the wall over her shoulder. The recurrent use in this first painting sequence of this cruciform shape points to its symbolic rather than decorative purpose. It is Madeline's bright, but failing defence against Roderick's diabolism. The candles by which Roderick paints her are only the first example of infernal illumination and consuming, destructive force (in 'The Oval Portrait' the light-source is a mere skylight). As Roderick sits glowering at the visitor and the doctor by the fire, the open hearth behind him smoulders high like lava. Over the hearth as mantel design is a swan with outspread wings and drooping neck.

Roderick bursts into life, gets rid of his visitor by sending him for a walk, and then lifting Madeline's black shawl to uncover his palette speeds to his work, the camera tracking in fast motion behind him. Outside, the visitor, on his walk through the murky landscape, encounters a black dog which he attempts to call to him. The dog runs off. The visitor is an old man, far older than any possible school-companion of Roderick, and his defective vision and hearing (as well as a magnifying glass he uses an ear trumpet), while contrasting well with Roderick's hyper-sensitivity, both make him a comic figure and one, like us, to whom through the seeing-aid of slow motion, the dramaturgy of time, the mystery will be revealed of the doom of the Ushers. In the context of other animals in the film (frogs and a cat) the dog is only one of the devil's disguises.

Inside the castle, Roderick, working by the glare of a bank of more than fifty candles, ruthlessly attacks his palette, Madeline reacting to the stabs of his brush as if to her face, but wilting also both in the intense heat and under Roderick's stare. She collapses, cinematically, in a series of superimposed images of her face which finally give way to a negative image which impresses us as a death-mask. The candles drip fiercely to the ground. Roderick revives her, tenderly kissing her hands. Outside, the bell in the tower is ringing, and the visitor takes it, comically, as a summons to return home. But actually it rings the moment of Roderick's final assault. Madeline topples and turns in slow motion (the arabesque of the dying swan) to the ground. The visitor returns to find Roderick rapt before the portrait. Retreating from its life-like aspect they stumble over Madeline's body. Immediately Roderick is carried with the camera fast towards us, and as he whirls in vertigo with her body in his arms, little fires start unaccountably to break out across the floor.

Roderick turns to his necromantic books, and by flickering candlelight searches for a remedy at her cataleptic death-bed where she lies with a star-fish shadow cast over her abdomen. Roderick descends a staircase of thorny posts linked with heavy chains, symbolic of the barren prison, the sterile tree of Usher. As the valet deliberately but incongruously carries a coffin upstairs, we see it first in normal motion and then from Roderick's subjective angle, in slow motion. The incongruous becomes oneiric, almost Surrealist. Roderick contemplates his portrait, raptures of joy giving way to expressions of grief, his face changing imperceptibly with the camera's speed, wholly justifying Epstein's theory.

Outside, a cortège makes its way down an avenue over which is superimposed an avenue of candles. Candles appear over the bridal veil which trails from the coffin, over Roderick's harrowed face, and over the bearers whose difficulties as they traverse the boggy ground are enacted by the lurching of a subjective camera. In a less malignant world an avenue of trees and candles might suggest a cathedral, but we have seen candles as the means by which Roderick has consumed Madeline's life, and the trees, now shot from below their branches, appear clawing, tearing, threatening to pluck the life out of all who pass under them. The veil blows away in a negative superimposition in analogy with the negative death-mask.

The burial chamber is a grotto, exotically decorated with flower and shell forms. Roderick, pushed reluctantly back up its steps by the visitor, looks longingly back as the wind ruffles his hair in the subtlest slow motion to see the doctor, who is supervising the nailing down of the coffin, moving his head and shoulders vigorously forward and back over it in a movement unconsciously simulating the sexual act as the hammer drives the nails into the lid. The overtone of the scene is confirmed by the extraordinary montage which follows. As Roderick and the visitor appear outside the grotto we have a sudden shot of two toads mating. Three elements are now rapidly inter-cut: Roderick and the visitor; the mating toads; and hammer blows falling faster and faster, multiplied in superimposition. A fourth element is added: an owl strangely illuminated in the undergrowth,which is inter-cut with the toads until Roderick and the visitor move away through the trees. In attributing this montage—wrongly, I think—to Buñuel, Francisco Aranda writes:

> What is admirable though is that these animals are presented in an activity which affirms life, as a counterpoint to the dead world which surrounds them and to the meaning which literary symbolism normally attributes to them. This sounds distinctly like a cry from Buñuel; and it is the kind of *trouvaille* that abounds in his later work.[1]

On the contrary, far from having a life-enhancing role to play the toads are enacting a sexual rite of the kind used in witchcraft to produce climactically an appearance of the devil as owl.

In the House of Usher a clock with pendulum is coming to the hour, a cat slinks between the feet of a suit of armour, curtains are moving in the wind and, inter-cut with these images, Roderick's guitar vibrates in sympathy as finally the clock strikes, the strings of the guitar snap and, as the whole house shakes (in superimposition), flashes of light spread across the film frame. A great wind rushes leaves before a tracking camera. On the wall beside the window is the image of a helmeted female with sightless eyes. Through the window, riven with lighting, Roderick points out to the terrified visitor an image of the owl. From outside we see a

---

[1] Francisco Aranda, *Luis Buñuel: A Critical Biography* (London, 1974), p. 41.

tree of stars towering over the house, a heavenly symbol of the Tree of Life with a small, stunted tree (the house itself) in the foreground. As Madeline returns from the grotto, two logs, seen in shot several times, at last fall apart and fire breaks out everywhere in the castle. Reunited, Roderick, Madeline and the entourage make their escape. They live again as the portrait burns. In the final frames of the film a cross appears in the sky next to the Tree of Life, and this is inter-cut with the image of the owl before the Christian image is imposed at the end.

From Buñuel's biographer we know that the Surrealist filmmaker, who in the next two years made *Un Chien Andalou* and *L'Age d'Or*, rejects any possible credit owing to him in Epstein's film. It is not difficult to see why. Epstein's version gives to Poe's story, a concern with God and the family which it never had. From Buñuel's point of view the happy ending, the finally purgative aspect of the destructive fires, the faith in a universal Tree of Life, carried the film away from his concept of the avant-garde back to the commercial cinema. The justification for Roderick and Madeline as a married couple comes with the incorporation of the story, 'The Oval Portrait'. A fortuitous by-product of this is that the potentially incestuous obsession of brother with sister of Poe's original is avoided. Epstein may have owned his own company but he was obviously looking for commercial distribution. Buñuel knew conventional bourgeois morality when he saw it. Epstein's substitution of the theme of fire for Poe's waters of the Tarn is a significant change. The fire which at first symbolizes Roderick's passion to consume Madeline's life for the sake of his art becomes a purgative force as it finally destroys the degenerate past of the House of Usher. Candle-power can be for good if represented by the stars in the firmament which form the Tree of Life. In passing, we should note that the Poe films directed by Roger Corman in Hollywood and England in the Sixties undoubtedly derive their climactic conflagrations and their satanic aspects from this early film by Epstein, and that three of them are thoroughly worthy of study: *The Haunted Palace* (1963), *The Masque of the Red Death* (1964) and *The Tomb of Ligeia* (1964). In 1951, two years before his death, Epstein was working on a new version of his film. The script is available to us (11: 265–331), and we find that he eliminated all the infernal aspects. He retained the married couple of 'The Oval Portrait' story but did away with the happy ending. Instead of the old visitor, with his still-life of magnifying glass, ear trumpet and fusty old books like the 'Mad Trist of Sir Launcelot Canning', we have a young dandy called Allan who reads Roderick anti-bourgeois satires like 'The Devil in the Belfry' and 'Lionizing', which, incidentally, Debussy and Mauclair liked respectively. But for all its updated ideology, there is no sign that in cinematic style the film was going to match his earlier masterpiece.

James Sibley Watson, Jr, born in 1894, was President of the Dial Publishing Company from 1919 to 1929. As such he was responsible for the best American literary magazine of its day, *The Dial*, edited by Marianne Moore in its last three years. Watson's interest in the cinema is plain from his editorial comment in the issue for February 1927. Having such a special involvement in the magazine, intellectually as well as financially, he would not have missed the articles on Poe at the time of the publication of Hervey Allen's biography, *Israfel*, which appeared that year. Watson, like Epstein, was a medical student, who graduated from New York University and later in life became a research professor of radiology. Filming his first independent production in Rochester, New York, so far from Paris and even New York city, no doubt he did not wish to be pretentious enough to call it 'avant-garde'. But his film more than meets his own definition of the amateur spirit ('the desire for sincerity and freshness of treatment'); it is an advanced aesthetic work with a sound critical point.[1] Watson's team consisted of himself as director and cinematographer (with some assistance from one Louis Siegel); Melville Webber as writer, designer and actor of the visitor's role; Watson's wife Hildegarde playing Madeline (we should note that in Epstein's version the part was played by Abel Gance's wife, Marguerite) and a Herbert Stern as Roderick. Webber, a painter and archaeologist, fancied himself a set designer, but after a while began to realize the irk-

[1] See George C. Pratt, *Spellbound in Darkness*, 2 vols. (Rochester, N.Y.,1966), 11: 426–30, for Watson's comments on the production.

some folly of painting wall-board. Perhaps they had read Ezra Pound on the need to cast off the Caligaresque influence by extending the method of Alvin Langdon Coburn's Vorticist photographs ('vortographs') to the film, as he was doing by lending Léger his shaving mirror for *Ballet Mécanique* (1925).[1] They, too, rejected décor for moving prisms of various shapes, and lights. Watson held the modernist view that

> each medium of expression can and should be isolated and purified just as a chemical compound is isolated in the laboratory. You say to yourself that the cinema is not theater or the dance, and certainly not the novel, and then you begin to wonder what it is. You think of camera tricks as essential, of oppositions of movement, changes in size, changes in lighting and sharpness, accelerations and contrasts of speed, distortions of shapes and perspectives.

His aim was 'to improve the flow of the picture, gathering force from scene, so as to make the spectator feel not with any particular hero or heroine as one does in a cheap novel, but to make him feel the whole piece like a piece of poetry'. Watson realized that camera and optical printer control were the cornerstones of this essentialist view of the medium. Epstein would have agreed, with the reservation that he was aiming for a dramatic rather than graphic effect. This difference is reflected in the running times of the films; Epstein's lasts fifty-five minutes, while Watson's runs for only sixteen minutes. Epstein is treating the whole story, and Poe in general, while Watson is, as it were, treating the poem within the story, 'The Haunted Palace'. It would not do to take Watson at his own estimate as amateur. His dry New England wit, his defensive mockery of the idea of a Rochester avant-garde, belie the fact that he knew of the latest film work in Europe from *Close-Up*, which was to become the most important film magazine of the next few years, the first appearance of which he noted in the pages of his *Dial*, where there were also references to Man Ray's latest films. When the film opened in New York in 1929 at

[1] See Ezra Pound, *The Dial* (March, 1923), p. 272; *The Exile* 4 (Autumn, 1928), p. 113.

the Film Arts Guild it was in a cinema which made provision for three-dimensional films of the kind of which Marcel Duchamp was dreaming.

In Watson's film the top-hatted visitor arrives on horseback at a castle with turrets prismatically multiplied. Synchromist images of revolving stairs are followed by a fissure cutting jaggedly through a paper screen to reveal Madeline smelling hyacinths. Approaching Roderick she places her hyacinths in a vase containing arum lilies on a table at which she sits down. A black-gloved hand at the left of the frame pours a drink from a white bottle. Whose hand is this? The two toast each other like lovers, the close-up of Madeline shows her sensuous enjoyment of the draught which has the instant effect of causing a superimposition of meat dish covers and coffins. A meat dish is now presented to her representationally, again by black-gloved hands, this time from the right of the frame. She draws back as the camera slowly rotates, tilting her backwards. Roderick, first framed between the two arum lilies, approaches his sister, leans solicitously over her. Fade. When the image is restored he is still in the same position. His solicitude has something of the perverse.

A soft-focus image of water with drops falling in it creates a blurred effect. The visitor arrives at a German Expressionist painting of a door. Bells ring in superimposition furiously. Madeline appears as if sleep-walking. The visitor's face, superimposed over the door, is cleft through nose, mouth and chin with a black line dividing it into two halves. Madeline appears to approach him but arrives at moving stairs. The image of the visitor is repeated after which, with stairs moving on both sides of the frame, Madeline is seen in the centre being driven into the ground by a hammer shadow. She collapses as endless stairs escalate, buckling and bending, and a stream of coffins float upside down into the frame.

The camera tilts Roderick over Madeline, overpowering her mentally rather than physically although the means by which this is suggested are spatial. The coffins fill the frame again. Madeline has her black veil removed by black-gloved hands which caress her eyes as they close them, run the length of her body to her bare feet over which is superimposed, as if by a hammer, an armorial seal. Hammer and gloves are thrown in slow motion into a corner. Significantly, the next shot is of Roderick. A series of images of Madeline's face, wipes interrupting them and recomposing them as multiplied faces, follows. Then Roderick is recumbent with prismatic effects playing about his head as Madeline's hand projects large and grasping from the depths of the frame in distorted perspective. Roderick in a double image of himself walks stiffly downstairs, his raised hand making imaginary hammer blows. The shadow of the visitor's hat dances on the wall. Three hats appear, Roderick in double image, Madeline and Roderick in multiple image. Madeline's hands raised as shadows form the arabesque of a harpy. A pile of books rises before Roderick and the top-hat bounces high in psychokinetic defiance of gravity.

A top-hatted figure whose face is not visible turns the pages of a book. The letters BEVT appear (letter A upside down), a sawing-in-and-out effect created by a prism produces the word CRVCK (A upside down), then the word in mirror-form breaking into abstract lines, then RIPPD (without the E) appears, and SKREAM (with K). Stairs criss-cross. Feet ascend the stairs and move in negative onto an escalator running in all directions to converge in abstract lines. Madeline pushes back the door, floats into the room in multiple image and falls upon Roderick. The visitor makes his escape as the house falls into an abstract image of the moon reflected in the water which whirls like a maelstrom, in reverse motion.

It has often been remarked that characterization is not the strength of Poe's tales. His leading men, Usher and William Wilson, and his ladies, Ligeia, Morella, Eleanora and Madeline, are shadowy figures. The minor characters in the story of Usher are quite indistinct. It allows Epstein—indeed, with his dramatic instincts, *makes* Epstein—suggest that the doctor is a potential body-snatcher with a taste for necrophilia, and that the visitor is an insensitive old fool with good intentions. But equally it allows Watson the perception that the visitor is none other than Roderick's double, the side of him that begs a former schoolfellow to rescue him from himself. The black gloves are those of the visitor, or Roderick's projection of himself. They pour the wine, uncover the meat dish, which drive Madeline into her cataleptic state. They caress her inert body, and are thrown down with the hammer, immediately after which we have a shot of Roderick. The identification between Roderick and the visitor is made purely visually, as one would hope in a silent film. There would be no need to hide the face of the top-hatted figure who turns the pages of the book if it were not intended to blend Roderick with the visitor. It is Roderick who reads too much. The visitor-narrator of the story is Roderick himself, witness of his own disintegration. The divided face of the visitor is the emblem of his divided self. Watson's recognition of the doppelgänger motif in the story was one which psychoanalytical approaches to Poe were beginning to explore. It is not my purpose to claim critical precedence for him, but to applaud the critical articulation of this psychological perception in creative form.

Both these films belong to a tradition of Poe criticism which is more French than Anglo-American. In the English-speaking world Poe had at this time either been ignored or dismissed; only D. H. Lawrence and William Carlos Williams had made creative use of him. Lawrence, like Munch although with more detachment, saw the story of Usher as a 'love' story:

Love is the mysterious vital attraction which draws things together, closer, closer together. For this reason sex is the actual crisis of love. For in sex the two blood-systems, in the male and the female, concentrate and come into contact, the merest film intervening. Yet if the intervening film breaks down, it is death.[1]

Williams, on the other hand, responded less to the subject matter than to Poe's method—the arbitrary choice of material, the rejection of American 'scenery', and the quality of his composition, 'proving even the most preposterous of his inventions plausible—that BY HIS METHOD he makes them WORK.'[2] These

[1] D. H. Lawrence, *Studies in Classic American Literature* (1923), (London, 1964), p. 62.
[2] W. C. Williams, *In the American Grain* (1925), (N.Y. 1953), p. 230.

reactions are essentially those of Baudelaire and Valéry respectively. But perhaps the most important contribution that these various artist-critics make in whatever medium—music, painting or film—is the place they give to 'The Fall of the House of Usher' in Poe's work. Twenty years later, in 1948, T. S. Eliot considered Poe's tales only in terms of their contribution to the rise of detective fiction, and thought the subject of 'The Haunted Palace' Poe's 'own weakness of alcoholism'—as if it were verse from some temperance society tract.[1] It may be that it is Poe's stories which constitute the body of work which eluded him in the form of the long poem. But Eliot's judgment that Poe is unscrupulous in language and immature in personality is the common one. The French interest in him is to be explained, said Eliot, because they identified with him as an outcast in society, used his theories to develop their own *poésie pure*, and did not know English very well. Lawrence, on the other hand, saw Poe as doomed to perform a necessary task for society: 'For the human soul must suffer its own disintegration, *consciously*, if it is ever to survive.'[2] The radical avant-garde in Europe and America have continued to appreciate his contribution to post-modernist aesthetics. As for not knowing English, perhaps this was what gave the French their edge. Poe's 'primitive awkwardness of diction', as Williams called it, came from his provincial American background, out of which we have gradually observed a distinctively American language emerge, and with it a rhetoric, a way of putting elements together, that is also remarkably American. Eliot's judicial criticism closes the mind on possibilities that Epstein's and Watson's creative criticism opens up. I should like to dedicate this grateful essay to Dr Watson in Rochester, and to the memory of Jean Epstein.

[1] T. S. Eliot, 'From Poe to Valéry' (1948), *Hudson Review* II, 3 (Autumn, 1949), p. 335.
[2] Op. cit., p. 61.

VIII

Theatre and History

CHRISTOPHER FRY

IN the theatre history means people rather than events. What they do is less important than what they feel and suffer while doing it. Their success or failure isn't measured in worlds conquered or lost, but in the private battlefield, in the vale of soul-making, as Keats called it. Certainly the human frailties and conflicts of a historical character also belong to the historian's business, but there they are necessarily seen and judged as a part of public affairs. To the playwright the social and political issues, interesting and important as they may be, are a part of the making or un-making of a man. The depth of feeling experienced in taking a decision is of greater moment than the decision's outcome, whether bad or good. The stature of a man is not the height he achieves (one man's easy reach is another man's Everest) but the quality of his effort to ascend. When writing about Henry II and Becket, it was not Becket's sainthood born of Church-and-State politics that chiefly concerned me, nor the evaluation of Henry's Customs of the Kingdom; it was the degree of self-deception in Becket's thrust, and the whole anguish of Henry's parry; so that I was driven to ask myself whether, by his dedicated suffering for an ideal (his Passion, in a religious sense), Henry was not the more saintly of the two. (It is the Tempters who give the dramatic significance to *Murder in the Cathedral*, not the blood of the blessed martyr or the Church triumphant in adversity; not what is done but what is suffered in doing it.)

If a play has anything to say about history which isn't better said by historians, it's in this close identification with the private man, and in revealing the matrix of his life which underlies the complex planes of his experience. The need to select, to contain a lifetime within two or three hours, has this advantage over the crowded pages of the historian: that we can glimpse the shape of the life, as a speeded-up ciné camera can show the pattern of movement in a growing plant. By bringing into close proximity what happened in a wide space of time, the theatre can take the God's-eye view, often ironic, but redemptive in its perception of form within apparent chaos. How much historical fact can be distorted for the sake of theatrical effectiveness is a matter of the playwright's conscience. I believe that keeping faith with the past is more important than the dividends to be got from unjustified flashes of 'good theatre'. They are small change compared with the realities of the human drama *sub specie aeternitatis.*

IX

'Meaning Motion': Old Music and Some Modern Writers

RICHARD LUCKETT

WHEN Ezra Pound visited Arnold Dolmetsch and heard 'a bewildering and pervasive music moving from precision to precision within itself' he knew that Dolmetsch was no longer, from a journalist's point of view, a 'topic'. Dolmetsch had first come to England thirty years earlier: since then he had inspired a novel by George Moore (*Evelyn Innes*, 1899) and a poem by Symons; he had excited the enthusiasm of Morris and Burne-Jones; his work had earned the warmest praise from Shaw; at Yeats's instigation he had made a psaltery for Florence Farr, though in 1904 he had not been able to oblige a Mr James Joyce, who wanted a lute with which to 'coast the south of England, singing old English songs'. In 1918 Pound was delighted when Joyce saw and approved his Dolmetsch clavichord. For Pound had espoused Dolmetsch's cause and urged his genius, not out of any concern for what was fashionable, but because he regarded Dolmetsch as the embodiment of a tradition upon which the health of poetry itself depended. In 1915, with the publication of *The Interpretation of the Music of the XVIIth and XVIIIth Centuries,* Dolmetsch had given literary shape to what Pound described as his 'wisdom'—a word that Yeats also had used when writing of Dolmetsch years before. Pound's tribute was the essay on '*Vers Libre* and Arnold Dolmetsch', which asserted the view, to which the book had helped him, that '*vers libre* exists in old music'. When he eventually composed Canto LXXXI (1945), Pound achieved a memorial that comprehended Dolmetsch's achievements as performer and craftsman as well:

> Has he tempered the viol's wood
> To enforce both the grave and the acute?
> Has he curved us the bowl of the lute?
>> *Lawes and Jenkyns guard thy rest*
>> *Dolmetsch ever be thy guest*

Pound's conviction, to which Dolmetsch so largely contributed, that 'poetry atrophies when it gets too far from music', was of the first importance for the development of his work. Yet, just as Pound was not alone amongst writers in his praise of Dolmetsch, so Dolmetsch was not alone amongst musicians in his discovery of those composers who had lived before Bach and Handel, and of the techniques proper to the performance of their music. The creation of 'the present moment of the past' that gave these composers their fresh significance was the work of many men, both scholars and amateurs, and much had been accomplished before Dolmetsch made his own important, but not decisive, contribution. Nor did the poets respond to Dolmetsch alone. In 1873, ten years before Dolmetsch's arrival, Hopkins had made detailed notes of the instruments to be seen in the South Kensington Museum. This collection, built up by Carl Engel, was later to suggest to Hardy his 'Haunting Fingers: a phantasy in a museum of musical instruments'—a poem as evocative in its references to the instruments as it is allusive in its Cecilian form. As amateur composer Hopkins was fascinated by the early scores that he studied, and in 1885 a pianist pleased him by remarking that his music seemed to date 'from a time before the piano was'. A distrust of the 'pyano' was to be a characteristic attitude of Pound's, and Yeats, contrasting the older instruments, responsive to the whole being, with their modern equivalent, observed that 'if you sit at the piano, it is the piano, the mechanism, that is the important thing, and nothing of you means anything but your fingers and your intellect'. Percy Lubbock expressed the same opinion another way when, in his study of Samuel Pepys (1909), he praised 'the lute, the viol and the harpsichord' as the 'severer trainers of taste'. Hopkins had appreciated the point earlier, just as he had anticipated Yeats's interest in declamation; these things were merely facets of the innate yet learned sympathy that enabled him to make his poem to Henry Purcell (1879), praising Purcell that 'whereas other musicians have given utterance to the moods of man's mind, he has, beyond that, uttered in notes the very make and species of man . . .'

The immediacy and seriousness of this poem can aid us in attempting a distinction between those reactions to the redis-covered world of old music which were creative, which contri-buted to a new order of masterpieces, and those which had more to do with taste than inspiration. The invocation of 'virginals and organs . . . psaltery . . . viol and harp' in Lionel Johnson's *A Song of Israel* (1889) is not intended to be more than decorative. By the end of the Great War old instruments had sufficient currency for it to seem appropriate that, when Bertrand Russell was released from prison for 'expressing unusual opinions about the war' Osbert Sitwell gave a party and Lady Ottoline Morell took him to hear Mrs Violet Gordon Woodhouse play the harpsichord. Mrs Woodhouse's playing was the subject of a poem by W. H. Davies, and Walter de la Mare tried, in a solitary mimetic quat-rain, to recapture the voice of a clavichord. These verses (and there are others, of less merit) simply reflected a state in which it was natural that Ellen Terry should own a spinet, and Eric Gill a clavichord. When David Jones pictured a clavichord (possibly Gill's?) in his 'English Window' (1931) he was, of course, implying something about the quietness, and also the range, of his own art. Yet he was within the bounds of realism: the revival of early music was bound to be reflected in literature and, to a lesser extent, painting. It was a process that had occurred even at a popular level. January 1891 saw the first issue of *The Early English Musical Magazine*, a periodical of surpassing vulgarity which acted as the organ of the 'Early English Music Society'. The magazine, though it gave glowing reports of Dolmetsch's activi-ties, had no connection with him. Readers were assured that the exploration of the rich treasury of vocal music would help them attain 'the most complete cultivation of the voice, and also that higher culture, the refinement and ennobling of the mind'. The relation of all this to what was fashionable and faddish is suggested by the information that a lecture-recital, held in St James Hall on 3rd April, was given at the invitation of the 'Balloon Society'. Nevertheless the music published in the magazine, though disfigured by bad accompaniments, included pieces by Purcell, Lawes, Blow, Morley, Byrd, Ravenscroft, Playford and Galliard. Mrs Emma Marshall's *In the Choir of Westminster Abbey: A Story of Henry Purcell's Days* (1897) must have appealed to a similar taste. As it happened Mrs Marshall had, through her husband, acquired considerable knowledge of some aspects of her subject, if not of others: '"Master Purcell knows what these quarter tones mean" . . . If Mr Purcell knew, I did not.' The revival was a fact of artistic life; its pedigree could be traced back at least to the foundation of Dr Pepusch's Academy of Vocal Musick in 1726, and it had gained ground steadily over a hundred and fifty years, until the original revivers were being revived in their turn. The idea that Hopkins's response to the old music was made possible by immediately contemporary scholarship can be controverted by even the most casual glance at the wealth of informed reference in Browning. Yet it is apparent that Hopkins's reactions differed from Browning's, and it is also apparent that, after 1880, the revival acquired a more radical emphasis.

One way of describing this emphasis would be to say that it derived from a new sense of the importance of the medium, of the material and texture of performance; another would be to say that it stemmed from acute dissatisfaction with the accepted conventions of composition. Both views imply a rejection of the naïvely evolutionary concept of music which underlay many nineteenth-century assumptions about the art, so that when G. A. Macfarren wished to commend Purcell, he none the less contrived to refer to his 'wonderful anticipation of modern harmony'. Before 1880 there were very few people who would have accepted Samuel Butler's view that music had actually been declining since the time of Handel, or would at all have understood his statement that modern music was not 'what I mean by music. It is playing another game and has set itself aims which, no doubt, are excellent but which are not mine'. It is hardly surprising that Butler welcomed Dolmetsch's concerts, and it is also relevant to note his criticisms of evolutionary theory. In so far as interest in early music before 1880 had had to do with large-scale choral works (and this was the main emphasis) it marched with the general tendencies of nineteenth-century composition and thus seemed less distinct than it might otherwise have done. After 1880, however, we find that it was small-scale works which most occupied those concerned with old music; in this respect Dolmetsch is as much exemplar as innovator.

The shift coincided with an increase in the attention paid to song, but the equation is not as straightforward as would at first appear. A. H. Bullen, for instance, who printed the texts of many of the best Elizabethan lyrics during the 1880s, was described by Yeats as a man 'who hates all music but that of poetry, and knows of no instrument that does not fill him with rage and misery'. Yet Bullen became an admirer of Florence Farr's declamation to the psaltery, and in 1902 published twelve lute ayres, with their settings transcribed by Janet Dodge, one of Dolmetsch's pupils (Joyce was a purchaser of this elegant volume). Here we find concurrent and allied enthusiasms going their separate ways for some twenty years before they reached their natural union. It must be regarded as something of a tragedy that Bullen and Dolmetsch never collaborated directly.

The case of Bullen serves as a warning against too simplified a reading of the revolution in taste that I have tried to summarize. It was in about 1870 that Macfarren said of Gibbons's *Fantazies of III Parts*:

> they would, it is true, be little congenial to modern ears, but this is because of the strangeness of the crude tonal system that prevailed at the time, and upon which they are constructed . . . Judged by the only true standard of criticism – judged merely as what they were designed to be – they must be pronounced excellent proofs of the musical erudition, the ingenious contrivance, and the fluent invention of the composer.

Macfarren seems to have been unaware of the paradox of his position, but his words aptly indicate a watershed; in the remaining years of the century 'strangeness' was to worry people much less, whilst a 'true standard of criticism' became more common.

Even today the conflict continues, though the forlorn hope of the old guard is heavily camouflaged. But the late nineteenth-century shift was sufficient for poets and writers to discover a world of music that answered to something they were beginning to feel as an urgent need, that gave to their experiments the sanction of ancient practice, whilst having a particular and liberating potency because this was expressed in an art-form other than their own. The consequence of the direct imitation of the literary text of an Elizabethan lyric would almost certainly be a worthless pastiche, but no such problem existed if the formal inspiration came from Elizabethan *music*. It is hardly a coincidence that Pound's tendency to pastiche diminished almost in proportion to the extent that he became involved with old music; he had found a new and better dependence.[1]

What the older music had to offer, to judge from the record of literary response, was immediacy, purity, informality and originality. It was emancipated from the mechanization of the nineteenth-century orchestra and free of the clotting tendencies of nineteenth-century harmony. Above all, it suggested that there were alternatives to the tyranny of quantitative accent. Whether these things were what the older music 'really' had to offer remains at least as open to question as, for example, the accuracy of Stravinsky's view of the essentially 'Classical' nature of the early eighteenth-century Italian instrumental concerto. But the implications of the older music for a sense of accent can hardly be doubted. In her *About Elizabethan Virginal Music* (1924) Margaret Glyn asserted that 'what we need to do is *to get rid of the accent*, not only the actual accent, but the *sense* of accent'. Peter Warlock, amplifying this in *The English Ayre* (1926), added the necessary qualification: what Margaret Glyn had meant was *quantitative* accent, for 'the real secret of the Elizabethans' success in welding

---

[1] There were, needless to say, other factors involved; but if the intervention of Ford Madox Ford is seen as crucial, then it has to be said that Ford, also, had learned much from Dolmetsch, and did so before the period of his close acquaintanceship with Pound.

verbal and musical phrases into a homogeneous whole is to be found in their clear realization that rhythm and metre are not identical'. For Warlock the essence of the good speaking of verse was the appropriate stress on 'the rhythms conditioned by the sense of the words, leaving the metre to the hearer's understanding', and this was also the essence of Elizabethan music.

Warlock was doing no more than reiterate a principle which was integral to Dolmetsch's approach, and which before that had been essential to the thinking of both Hopkins and Robert Bridges. But to mention these two last names in this context is to introduce a note of caution. Bridges was a fine practical musician, a close friend of that remarkable scholar of polyphony, H. Ellis Wooldridge, and a professed lover of 'the purer style'. In 1924 Bridges' admirers could think of no better way to please him than by presenting him with a Dolmetsch clavichord. His essays on 'English Chanting' in *The Musical Antiquary* reveal how he could unite his musical and poetic skills in order to illumine a complex subject. His *Ode to Music* for the Purcell Bicentenary Commemoration (1895), together with its preface, testifies to the practical and creative application of these skills. Yet Bridges fully accepted Hopkins's position (put to him in a letter of May, 1885) that 'even given the genius, a musician must be that and nothing else, as music now is'; and despite Bridges' greater musical competence, he was far less ready than Hopkins to adapt the lessons of the one art to the other. Hopkins sought wholly to dispense with Parnassian quantitatives: Bridges endeavoured to restore a proper sense of stress without abandoning the metrical line. For both procedures there were purely literary precedents: Hopkins could point to Early English models, and Bridges to the example of Milton. We cannot posit any simplistic causal relationship between the new musical understanding and the new emphasis on stress in poetry; the only poet for whom such a case might conceivably be made out is Pound, and for Pound early music seems to have been a clarifying and sustaining—rather than directly innovatory—force. What we can observe, however, is an interdependence, a creative exchange, involving not only two arts, but also several centuries.

Yet this does not make it unprofitable to speculate as to which, amongst arts and periods involved, 'was the mooste fre'. The earlier centuries had no option but to give to the later, and if the nineteenth century, by its excesses, added a particular lustre to the past, then this too was an accidental generosity. The masterpiece exists as the masterpiece; to consider the possibility that the renewed appreciation of Purcell was at root a function of an alteration in nineteenth-century poetic practice is to confront the absurdity of a wholly relativist view of taste. But what does emerge is that the ordering of the arts has a bearing here. The literary masterpiece is subject to those vagaries of language attendant on time and place. The visual arts and music are not in the same degree sensitive to these vagaries. They depend on the various grammars that control them, and music is undoubtedly more subject to national and temporal inflection than painting. Yet it still remains a thing in itself, immutable in a way that the work of literature is not, though accordingly restricted. An event at the turn of the century illustrates something of this aspect of a musical masterpiece, and also suggests the ramifications of creative exchange: I mean the production, by Edward Gordon Craig and Martin Shaw, of Purcell's *Dido and Aeneas*.

This amateur venture, mounted in a small Hampstead concert hall, and performed three times only, has a claim to be considered the most influential theatrical event of the last hundred years. It introduced new principles of staging, lighting and scenic abstraction, and these were eventually to influence the content of modern theatre as decisively as they had initially influenced its form. Martin Shaw, who had only recently left the Royal College of Music (where he felt that he had learnt little), was a passionate lover of Purcell, Bach, Gregorian chant and English folk-song; he originally envisaged a concert performance of the opera, but was convinced by Craig that it must be staged. His enthusiasm was entirely his own, but it is fair to note that without the work of the 'Musical Antiquarian Society' and the 'Purcell Society', both organizations which were part of that long-term and historic rediscovery of early music which I have tried to indicate as the foundation for the more dramatic revival after 1880, Shaw might not have known the work at all. As it was, his vision of it fired Craig, who wrote that 'on the music we were entirely in agreement —so that what he felt I felt'. It was this unanimity that enabled Craig to give full expression to his gifts in the production. The consequences are well enough known, and have been documented by historians of the stage. What has not been properly appreciated is Purcell's part: the Hampstead *Dido* was the only wholly satisfactory production that Craig achieved,[1] and though it is easy to find purely practical reasons for the failure of his later projects, a contributory factor in each case was the nature of the work he was trying to produce. If he had ever staged Bach's *St Matthew Passion*, as he hoped, it might have succeeded; certainly the absolute nature of opera and oratorio reduced the possibility of the wrangling that damaged the Moscow Arts Theatre *Hamlet* and the Lessing Theatre *Venice Preserved*, and it is a part of my point here that Craig was an original artist, and that though he was humble before his texts his humility was that of one great artist confronted by another's masterpiece; it was not the professional subordination of the good producer. Yet for Craig that single opera was sufficient, and the encounter realized in him the gifts that in their turn inspired Yeats and Reinhardt, Isadora Duncan and Meyerhold.

A *metteur-en-scène*, who must translate art into a dependant art, is clearly susceptible to the influence of a masterpiece in some ways that a poet is not, whilst a poet, who has a different kind of responsibility to the masterpieces he may encounter, is free to enact his response in his own art. As I have suggested, Craig is an exceptional example, and has to be seen as more than a producer. In Pound's phrase 'one art interprets another'; Purcell enabled Craig to break through the level of the 'theatrical', and this was exactly what Pound had to say about Dolmetsch's re-creation of ancient dance—though this re-creation was scrupulously historic, whilst Craig made no concessions to seventeenth-century conventions, whether of movement or décor. It was Purcell's energy, his immediacy of expression, that moved Craig to the creation of a new theatrical idiom, and if we wish to recreate something of

---

[1] A partial exception might be made for *The Masque of Love* in the next year, but this was of course Purcell's masque in *Dioletian*.

what Craig must have felt in Purcell we can do so by turning to Hopkins's poem. Now both Hopkins and Craig might have felt as fervently about Shakespeare (and all the evidence suggests that they did), yet Shakespeare's place in theatrical and literary tradition prevented his calling forth the wholeness of response that we can test in Hopkins's poem, and infer from our knowledge of Craig.

The 1900 *Dido and Aeneas* is an extreme example, but none the less valuable for that. The literary influence of the 'rediscovery' of early music can be traced far beyond Hopkins and Bridges, Yeats and Pound. There were many factors that exercised a common but independent influence on this rediscovery and on the new directions of English (and American) poetry. But there are also points at which we can discern, clearly enough, the masterpiece transcending time, place, and the frontiers between the arts. And beyond that the re-entry of forgotten masterpieces into the canon of music modified (or confirmed, as I suspect is the case with Hopkins) the 'imagined music' which Pound saw as informing all living poetry. For musicians the matter was not so simple: they were not preserved, by the separation of the arts, from the dangers of pastiche and derivation. Nor could they have the writer's recourse to the omnivorous eclecticism of literary expression. In this important respect literature, to my mind the least generous party in these transactions, was nevertheless in the modern, not the Chaucerian sense—more 'free'.

X

Criticism and the Religious Prospect

NATHAN A. SCOTT, JR

OURS is a period in which—most especially as the *nouvelle critique* (of Barthes and Derrida and Foucault) begins more and more to invade Anglo-American forums—a very considerable piety supports collaborations between literary criticism and such extraneous disciplines as psychoanalysis, cultural anthropology, the sociology of knowledge, and various forms of 'post-critical' social-political theory. Yet, for all its new eagerness to explore the manifold extramural affiliations in which literature is entangled, the conventional English-department mentality in university circles seems generally committed to its old reluctance to acknowledge the possibility that the study of literature may necessarily trench upon orders of valuation that are essentially religious; and thus the discipline of theology is not generally considered to be one in which criticism may find a useful resource. Indeed, Mrs Leavis's verdict of a generation ago is still that which is likely to be handed down by the average don:

> There is no reason to suppose that those trained in theology
> . . . are likely to possess what is essential to the practice of
> literary criticism, that 'sensitiveness of the intelligence' described
> by Matthew Arnold as equivalent to conscience in moral
> matters. A theological training seems to have a disabling effect
> and has subsequently to be struggled against when literary
> criticism is the concern.[1]

Despite, however, the animus with which the professional arbiters customarily regard any collaboration between criticism

[1] Q. D. Leavis, 'Charlotte Yonge and "Christian Discrimination"', *Scrutiny,* Vol. 12, No. 2 (Spring, 1944), p. 158.

and a religious perspective, it is just such an affiliation that has promoted in recent years, at least on the American scene, a notable insurgency that has found expression in numerous conferences and symposia and in a remarkable spate of publication.

Within the theological community this is an insurgency that has been very largely prompted by a growing recognition of how tenuous must be any definition of the Christian faith that fails adequately to measure the constancy with which it has at once leavened and been leavened by those agencies of culture of which the literary enterprise is the chief organ. The novelist and the dramatist and the poet may, of course (as I have elsewhere remarked), 'help the theological imagination to *see* how this or that particular faith or life-orientation really *looks*, under the full stress of experience'.[1] But, then, as the living issues of religion (sin and penitence and forgiveness and grace and reconciliation and despair and hope) are enacted and dramatized in poetic literature, inevitably the basic categories and structures of formal theology come to be tested and challenged by the metamorphic processes of art, so that, in one or another moment of the literary tradition, the funded inheritance of religious thought is by way of being revised and complicated and extended in many complex and subtle respects. Which is to say that, again and again, the literary imagination, through its capacity for creative transformation of our received 'world-hypotheses', proves to be a genuinely innovative and renewing force in the world of religious meanings. The conventional histories of theological doctrine tend to present the Christian faith as if it had always been merely an affair of formal doctrine, but in point of fact the full actuality of its various historical modes can never, finally, be explicated with any proximate adequacy unless the most careful attention is paid to the multifarious expressions that this faith has won in cultural forms. One may, for example, study the vicissitudes of Evangelicalism in the English nineteenth century by scanning the relevant theological treatises and documents, but it is unlikely that what is genuinely

---

[1] Nathan A. Scott, Jr, 'Introduction: Theology and the Literary Imagination' in Nathan A. Scott, Jr (ed.), *Adversity and Grace: Studies in Recent American Literature* (University of Chicago Press, Chicago, 1968), p. 22.

decisive here will be deeply appropriated, apart, say, from the fiction of George Eliot, apart from such books as *Adam Bede*, *Middlemarch*, *The Mill on the Floss* and *Scenes of Clerical Life*. Or, again, the event that was comprised by the sudden burst upon the European scene in 1919 of Karl Barth's *Der Römerbrief* is an event that can in various ways be located within the developing history of modern theology and that can thus be accounted for and to some extent understood. But the peculiar violence of feeling and rhetoric that are so much a part of the phenomenon presented by this epoch-making book will not be very deeply comprehended, if one has no lively awareness of the cultural world by which Barth had been formed—which was not simply the world of Troeltsch and Harnack and Herrmann but also the world that is dramatically presented, say, in the fiction of Dostoievski and the theatre of Ibsen and Strindberg and the poetry of Rilke and von Hofmannsthal. Moreover, there is virtually no major episode in the history of theology about which similar notations are not to be made, most especially so in relation to the theological ferment occasioned over the past quarter-century by the generation of Bultmann and Tillich. And thus—to say nothing of the large and obvious ways in which Christian thought has shaped and informed literary tradition—the deeply fecundating role of modern literature in the life of theology has led the theological community increasingly in recent years to sponsor numerous studies of what appears most fundamentally to be at stake in the testimonies that come from the major writers of the age.[1]

Nor have critics confessedly allegiant to a theological perspective been without many counterparts among those who do not own such a commitment but whose actual work is no less guided by religious interests. And in this there is no cause for surprise, for the literature of the modern movement—which embraces not only Yeats and Kafka, not only Baudelaire and Dostoievski, but also Blake and Leopardi and Vigny and Heine—is a canon which, having taken unto itself a large pedagogic authority in relation to the ultimate mysteries of the world, is drenched in religious passion. Leslie Fiedler declared many years ago that criticism is

[1] See Appendix, p. 109.

perforce 'always becoming "something else"', for the simple reason
that literature is always "something else"'[1]—which is a dictum that
very nearly describes the fate of any critical enterprise devoted to
the great central texts of the modern tradition. For they constitute
a literature whose intentions are scriptural, and a literature which
can therefore be reckoned with only as the interpreter consents, at
last, not only to be himself addressed by, but also in turn to address
his text—by confronting it with his own history, his own self-
understanding, his own living present. Indeed, it is just such a
dialectical interplay between interpreter and text that comprises
the special kind of hermeneutical event called forth by much of
the most characteristic literature of the modern period. And the
critic being thus required, at no small cost of comfort, to be at
once interrogated and also himself to make his own independent
testimony, it ought not to occasion surprise that his discourse has
so frequently bristled with theological rhetoric—as in Murray
Krieger's discussions of modern tragedy in *The Tragic Vision*,[2] or
J. Hillis Miller's studies of representative Victorians in *The
Disappearance of God*,[3] or M. H. Abrams' great book of 1971 on the
Romantic movement, *Natural Supernaturalism*,[4] or Ihab Hassan's
exposition of 'postmodernism' in *The Dismemberment of Orpheus*.[5]

Yet, for all the variousness of critical work exemplifying the
fruitfulness that may be approached by way of a criticism which
is open to the religious horizons of modern literature, ours is not
a moment conducive to any clear reckoning, at the level of basic
principle, with this whole range of consideration. For, quite apart
from the academy's old wariness about any room being made in
the field of criticism for a religious interest, the new avant-garde
resulting from the impact of recent European theory on Anglo-
American circles is so desperately confused about the nature of
literature and the mission of criticism as to be quite unprepared to

---

[1] Leslie Fiedler, 'Toward an Amateur Criticism', *The Kenyon Review*, Vol. 12,
No. 4 (Autumn, 1950), p. 564.
[2] Holt, Rinehart and Winston, New York, 1960.
[3] Harvard University Press, Cambridge, 1963.
[4] W. W. Norton and Col, New York, 1971.
[5] Oxford University Press, New York, 1971.

propose any clarifying account of the relevant issues. Under the tutelage of such theorists as Michel Foucault, Roland Barthes and Jacques Derrida, and with gestures in the direction of Saussure and Lévi-Strauss, the new scholiasts commit themselves to a fetishism of *le texte* more radical even than that fostered by the most inordinately formalistic versions of the New Criticism: yet, curiously, it is a fetishism calculated finally to rob the text of any kind of privileged status. For, as the American critic Edward Said declares: '*Everything* . . . is a text—or . . . *nothing* is a text.'[1] Which *means* that a work of literary art is merely type and example of the myriad ways whereby man—through styles of courtship and rituals of marriage, through special manners of eating and rituals of sport, through certain forms of economic transaction and methods of burying the dead—seeks to confer meaning on human existence by containing it within systems of signs; and, viewed from this perspective, *any* system of signs is a text, and a literary text is merely a system of signs. Wherever, in other words, man touches the world, there some form of textuality is to be found: indeed, from this standpoint, all the realities of culture are but expressions of the figurative impulse, of man's felt need to try, however vainly, to subdue the meaninglessness of the world by encircling it within systems of figuration, between none of which any significant evaluative discriminations are to be made. And it is just here that there arises the great difficulty that the *nouvelle critique* has unembarrassedly prepared for itself, for, since literature is dissolved into language and language into signs, its fetishism of the text, in nullifying any possibility of identifying the distinctively *literary* aspect of a literary text, proves at last to be of a kind that annihilates literary art: criticism becomes merely a department of semeiotics, and, since all signs merely fumble at the irremediable muteness of the world, the new scholiasts find themselves in the end needing to announce that criticism is ultimately absurd and beyond recall.

So it would seem, then, that we are now rapidly moving far away from the dispensation which Cleanth Brooks, Allen Tate,

[1] Edward W. Said, *Beginnings: Intention and Method* (Basic Books, New York, 1975), p. 338.

W. K. Wimsatt and the other leading spokesmen for the New Criticism instituted a generation ago. For that whole effort was dedicated to setting up great walls fencing off the verbal arts from everything that appeared to be related to them in only an 'extrinsic' way, and the reigning passion was for specifying the respects wherein (as it was phrased in T. S. Eliot's famous dictum) 'poetry is poetry and not another thing'. But the *nouvelle critique* being ushered in by contemporary Structuralism, as it finds 'textuality' in sexual mores and sports and politics and economics, seems bent on collapsing poetics altogether into linguistics and sociology and the other sciences of culture. In the one case art was utterly separated from 'life', and in the other no significant distinctions at all seem any longer possible. And, of course, neither perspective yields any good basis on which to assess the various interdisciplinary commitments (whether from the side of religious thought or from any other field) that beckon literary criticism.

In his autobiography of 1967, *Making It*, Norman Podhoretz at a certain point recalls an occasion on which William Phillips, the editor of the *Partisan Review*, 'once told the New Left-minded English critic Kenneth Tynan that he could not argue with him about politics, because Tynan's arguments were so old that he, Phillips, could no longer remember the answers.'[1] And the evidence would suggest that most of us in the critical community today suffer something like Mr Phillips's embarrassment of not being quite able to call to mind just how the course of critical theory in our time may be newly straightened. But surely, whatever may be the route that leads to the necessary reconstruction, the end to be sought is one that will involve some reinstatement of the traditional vision of literature as one of the great ways of reckoning with What Is. Few, of course, are likely now to suppose that there is any simple possibility of redeeming mimeticist doctrine in anything resembling its primitive or classical forms. For in our own late post-Kantian time we know man to be (in Cassirer's phrase) an *animal symbolicum*[2] who dwells most essentially

---

[1] Norman Podhoretz, *Making It* (Random House, New York, 1967), p. 319
[2] See Ernst Cassierer, *An Essay on Man* (Yale University Press, New Haven, 1944), chapter 2.

not in a world of Things but in a world of symbolic forms. And even the most intrepid defender of mimeticist theory on the modern scene, the late Ronald Crane, when he undertook in his Alexander Lectures at the University of Toronto to specify the nature of the object which the poem imitates, declared it to be something

> internal and hence strictly 'poetic' in the sense that it exists only as the intelligible and moving pattern of incidents, states of feeling, or images which the poet has constructed in the sequence of his words by analogy with some pattern of human experience such as men have either known or believed possible, or at least thought of as something that ought to be.[1]

Which was in effect for Crane to forswear any merely 'representationalist' view of literary art as an affair of copying or reproducing what is already *out there*. But Casserer himself, like every other theorist who has not been content to settle for some form of sheer subjectivism, was careful to insist, because he felt so required by the evidence, that art, together with all the great symbolic forms, though not a mere imitation or repetition of something already given, is yet a vehicle of 'true and genuine discovery'. 'The artist', as he says for example, 'is just as much a discoverer of the forms of nature as the scientist is a discoverer of facts or natural laws.'[2] And, in a time when the poem is thought of either as something utterly self-contained and autotelic or as merely a system of signs wherein (to use Saussure's terms) *le signifiant* (the signifier) and *le signifié* (the signified)[3] are essentially identical, it is precisely the *ontological* status of the verbal arts that awaits reaffirmation, albeit in a way that preserves a sense of the incommutable uniqueness of the poem *qua* poem.

But now, of course, that version of the world, of 'reality', which is embodied in a given poem or novel and which bids for our

---

[1] R. S. Crane, *The Languages of Criticism and the Structure of Poetry* (University of Toronto Press, Toronto, 1953), p. 56.

[2] Ernst Cassierer, op. cit., p. 143.

[3] Ferdinand de Saussure, *Course in General Linguistics*, trans. Wade Baskin (McGraw-Hill, New York, 1966), pp. 65ff.

imaginative assent, is to be found always something radically perspectival. In 'the world of Dostoievski' people talk and act in a certain way, just as they laugh and weep and love in accordance with a logic that is distinctively a part of this system of things. In 'the world of Proust', the modulations of speech and styles of action represented by Swann and Charlus and Odette and Mme Verdurin are controlled by still another logic which is indigenous to the world of the Vinteuils and the Guermantes. And so it is with 'the world of Wordsworth' or 'the world of Chekhov' or 'the world of Mann': each is sustained by its own causality and is obedient to its own 'metaphysic': the fictional personages making up each universe suffer in a certain way, think and dream and hate and pray in a certain way—which is ordained by the causalities peculiar to the given 'world'. And we begin to define the meaning of *Mansfield Park* or *The Portrait of a Lady* or *The Good Soldier* as we begin to define the special causality controlling thought and action and feeling in the world of Jane Austen or Henry James or Ford Madox Ford, the 'world' of each 'describing' our own in the degree to which it lights up (by a complex analogical process) the diverse forces by which we ourselves are moved and with which we must deal.[1]

'Really, universally,' said Henry James, 'relations stop nowhere, and the exquisite problem of the artist is eternally but to draw, by a geometry of his own, the circle within which they shall happily *appear* to do so.'[2] And it is the manner in which this circle is drawn, as it involves the writer's way of managing the formal resources of his medium (whether it be verse or fiction or drama), which discloses that which any humane criticism wants finally most to clarify—namely, the ruling perspective whereby those issues of human experience at the fore in a particular body of work are resolved.

This is, of course, a perspective, whatever it may prove to be in a given case, that reflects a certain habit of loyalty to some

---

[1] The drift of the previous paragraph is influenced by an unpublished paper of Professor Edward Wasiolek of the University of Chicago.

[2] Henry James, *The Art of the Novel: Critical Prefaces* (Charles Scribner's Sons, New York, 1934), p. 5.

discovered method of construing experience, and, even more, it reflects those most fundamental beliefs, those ultimate concerns, that offer the imagination a hierarchy of value and a kind of platform on the basis of which it may ferret out 'the figure in the carpet'. But, then, as I remarked on a previous occasion,

> . . . what is most essentially distinctive of the religious imagination is not its embrace of this or that particular religious system or its quest of some other world but its concern to understand *this* world in relation to issues of ultimate meaning and value. The drama of our worldly life may, of course, be found to be illuminatingly 'thematized' by the myths and symbols of a particular religious system; but what is of the essence of the religious consciousness is not an affair of its symbology but of its concern to apprehend the realities of our human world in relation to a region of things where all value and meaning are ultimately grounded. It might well be said perhaps that, in so far as man is a 'religious' creature, he is so by virtue of his preoccupation with 'the dimension of ultimacy'. Which is precisely what the English philosopher Stephen Toulmin is suggesting when he proposes that we consider reflection to be moving into a 'religious' dimension just in the degree to which it focuses on 'limiting questions', on questions having to do not with particular aspects of our moral or political or intellectual experience but with the ultimate foundations of all our valuing and acting and thinking – for this, as Professor Toulmin maintains, is most essentially the field of religious thought.[1]

Indeed, the insistence that came over and again from the most creative and widely influential theologian of this century, the late Paul Tillich, was to the effect that religion, 'in the largest and most basic sense of the word, is ultimate concern': religious reflection, in other words, entails nothing more nor less than the attempt to think about the concrete issues of our lives in relation to whatever it is that concerns us *ultimately* because it is considered itself to

[1] Nathan A. Scott, Jr, 'Criticism and the Religious Horizon,' in Howard Hunter (ed.), *Humanities, Religion, and the Arts Tomorrow* (Holt, Rinehart and Winston, New York, 1972), p. 54.

belong to the order of ultimacy.[1] And thus, as he contended, at whatever points a truly ultimate concern discloses itself in cultural materials—whether in poetic literature or the visual arts or philosophic systems—there, a kind of testimony is being made which asks, even if only implicitly, to be *placed* in relation to some order of essentially religious meaning. Which is not, of course, to say, in the case of the verbal arts, that all literature is informed by some sort of positively religious vision of the world, for any such allegation would be manifestly absurd. But, under such a perspective as Tillich's, it may be maintained that the literary imagination, in so far as it manages to transmute the sheer plenitude of the world into something like what Clive Bell long ago called 'significant form',[2] does so by virtue of some scale of importance and ultimacy—and what needs also to be said is that, in this whole process, serious literature (in its comic or tragic modes) tends inevitably, at least, to broach the kinds of issues that invite from criticism an essentially theological response. So, if religion is not primarily an affair of special myths and cultic systems but rather of any and every effort of the imagination to reckon with the full stretch of experience in *the dimension of ultimacy*, and if this is an effort underlying all cultural enterprise, then the real locus of religious meaning in literary art requires to be thought of not in terms of the iconological material deriving from a particular tradition of faith—which may or may not be present (and often is not) in a particular poem or novel: on the contrary, under the perspective being here advanced, any work of poetic art, however insistently 'secular' may be its affirmations, will be found open to some order of religious valuation, in the degree to which it shows itself to be ordered by some ruling perspective that has the character of what Tillich calls 'ultimate concern'. And it is, therefore, in the terms of such a rationale as this that the new insurgencies in criticism reflecting a religious interest will find their sanction.

It is only, of course, the zealot bent on hawking his special

[1] Paul Tillich, *Theology of Culture* (Oxford University Press, New York, 1964), pp. 7–8.
[2] See Clive Bell, *Art* (Chatto and Windus, London, 1914), chapter I.

sectarianism who will want to conceive the discipline of literary criticism as merely a department of theology, but the rest of us are not likely to forget that, as a distinctive type of *Wissenschaft*, it has its own unique procedures and its own irreducible autonomy as a field of intellectual work. Yet, since the world is a seamless garment and since therefore the opportunities for fruitful collaboration amongst the various branches of humanistic studies are manifold, there may be some merit in seeking to clarify, at the level of basic principle, what it is in the nature of literary art that legitimizes (*pace* Mrs Leavis!) the collaboration between criticism and a religious perspective.

Since today, unhappily, the personnel of the critical community is not generally drawn from those splendidly *un*common readers outside the academy whom Virginia Woolf modestly proposed to call 'common', my own conviction is that the general current of ideas in contemporary criticism might eventually be much enlivened if those supervising university doctoral programmes in literature were to introduce, as one phase of the examination requirements for the young ordinand, the prescript that he or she, in the field of his or her special interests, demonstrate the capacity to think about literature in the context of some non-literary discipline, whether it be politics or psychology or philosophy or the history-of-ideas, or something else. For it is such an exaction that would be calculated to convey to the young aspirant what he or she perhaps most needs to know, that the critic who wants to be something more than a comma-counter had better be able to bring *some* kind of systematic vision of the world to the study of literature—which, if it is a literature serious enough to repay rigorous study, wants to be in some sort of serious dialogue with its reader. And thus the final import of what I have said is intended to suggest that, in such an interdisciplinary transaction, theology (as it undertakes, in one or another of its versions, to offer a developed hermeneutic wherewith various patterns of religious meaning may be interpreted) is a discipline which Mrs Leavis and her numerous confreres of diverse allegiances ought not to be permitted summarily to rule out of court.

APPENDIX (see footnote, p. 100)

Of the many collections of essays that have appeared the following may be cited as representative: *The New Orpheus: Essays toward a Christian Poetic*, ed. Nathan A. Scott, Jr (Sheed and Ward, New York, 1964); *The Climate of Faith in Modern Literature*, ed. Nathan A. Scott, Jr (Seabury Press, New York, 1964); *Literature and Religion*, ed. Giles B. Gunn (Harper and Row, New York, London, 1971); and *Religion and Modern Literature: Essays in Theory and Criticism*, eds. G. B. Tennyson and Edward E. Ericson, Jr (Wm. B. Eerdmans Co., Grand Rapids, Mich., 1975). And the following may be cited as representative of the numerous volumes in this field by single authors: David Baily Harned, *Theology and the Arts* (Westminster Press, Philadelphia, 1966); William F. Lynch, S. J., *Christ and Apollo: The Dimensions of the Literary Imagination* (Sheed and Ward, New York, 1960); Nathan A. Scott, Jr, *The Broken Center: Studies in the Theological Horizon of Modern Literature* (Yale Univesity Press, New Haven, 1966); Nathan A. Scott, Jr, *Craters of the Spirit: Studies in the Modern Novel* (Sheed and Ward, London, 1969); Nathan A. Scott, Jr, *Negative Capability: Studies in the New Literature and the Religious Situation* (Yale University Press, New Haven, 1969); Nathan A. Scott, Jr, *The Wild Prayer of Longing: Poetry and the Sacred* (Yale University Press, New Haven, 1971); Nathan A. Scott, Jr, *Three American Moralists – Mailer, Bellow, Trilling* (University of Notre Dame Press, Notre Dame, 1973); Nathan A. Scott, Jr, *The Poetry of Civic Virtue – Eliot, Malraux, Auden* (Fortress Press, Philadelphia, 1976); and Amos N. Wilder, *The New Voice: Religion, Literature, Hermeneutics* (Herder and Herder, New York, 1969). Norman R. Cary's *Christian Criticism in the Twentieth Century* (Kennikat Press, Port Washington, N.Y., 1975) offers a useful survey of the entire field.